LOVE WITHOUT STRIFE

OLUFUNKE SIMBO SAGBUWA

৪৩৫৪৩

All scriptural quotations are from the Authorised King James Version and New King James version of the Holy Bible, except otherwise stated.

For further information, enquiries; please write or contact: Tel.: +234-803 315 4148,
+234-7043005558

First Published, September 2020

ISBN: 978-978-984-704-4

National Library of Nigeria
cataloguing-in- publication data
Imprint: Imperial Legacy Nig. Ltd.
Tel: +234-8033374137

Dedication

This book is fully dedicated to my healer, God the Father, the Son, and the Holy Spirit, who showed me mercy and called me into the ministry, providing the powerful inspiration and idea to write this book.

The glory and dedication of this book cannot be shared with any man.

Acknowledgment

Firstly, I acknowledge the Almighty God who gave me the inspiration to write this book.

I appreciate my father in the Lord, a man of grace, love, and honour, Late Pastor Olu Obanure, Former Assistant General Overseer (Admin and Personnel) of the Redeemed Christian Church of God, and his wife. I am greatly indebted to him for the role he played when he flew from Ghana to spend four hours in my house to attend to my case. This will remain ever green in my memory.

I also appreciate him, along with Pastor (Dr). Dan Ogun, for seeing the zeal and potential in me and giving me the first opportunity in a Pastoral role in the Redeemed Christian Church of God in 1999.

I appreciate my husband, Pastor Victor Sagbuwa, a man of prayer and faith, who stood by me and took his ground against the plague that wanted to attach itself to my life. It was a silent battle. You are indeed God-sent to be my husband.

My senior co-laborers in the Redeemed Christian Church of God, Late Elijah Daramola, and His amiable wife, Pastor Dele Babade, Pastor Olajide Oluwajobi, Pastor Joseph Olagbadegun, Pastor Nosa Ukponmwan and Pastor Ola Olademehin, were not left out in the victory. Thank you, sirs/ma. Pastor Zac Ade, my zonal Pastor at the time, who refused to give up on me. You are the best.

I specially appreciate all my team members of Turnaround Life Foundation and the Ministry who diligently follow me from one community to another to impact lives. God bless you for your passion for souls.

While space will not permit me to mention names, I thank everyone who might have had an input in the production of this book. I thank you all. God bless you.

TABLE OF CONTENTS

INTRODUCTION

Love is not a choice but a command from God. God views love seriously. Why? It is very important to our Christian journey and a determinant of many things in the kingdom. Love defines our level of relationship or association with God. And where there is no relationship, connecting and walking with God becomes a problem. All efforts and hours spent in quiet time, spiritual retreats, prayer and fasting become futile.

The importance of loving God and others cannot be over emphasized. Jesus said in John 13:34, *"A new commandment I give unto you, that ye love one another; as I have loved you, that ye also love one another."*

When you walk in love like the Messiah, you allow the unhindered flow of God's blessings to flow in your direction and begin to walk in the light of the word of God. But whenever you step out of the command of God to love, you will stumble, begin to shrink, sink, and walk in darkness. You will begin to take wrong steps that may eventually lead to failure.

As a sincere believer who desires a continuous flow of the presence of God, desires to do exploits for Him in supernatural ways, and to be above every situation, you require the keys of love as access.

When you have the keys to your house, you don't struggle to open your doors. Love is the force and key that makes you operate supernaturally without stress and shame. The force of love compels a believer to do good rather than evil. Believers are struggling with sins today because they don't operate fully in love; the more loving you become, the less sin you commit.

Love is a defence. It has the ability to deliver you from sin and protects you from sinning continuously. Nobody wants to offend whom he loves. When you are born again, you must have the consciousness that a greater one dwells in you and He makes you to resist sin.

1 John 4:4 says, "Ye are of God, little children, and have overcome them: because greater is he that is in you, than he that is in the world."

The Spirit of God which resides in you is the same Spirit that enables you to love people. God's nature is love, not hate; you must therefore practice love all the days of your life if you want to walk with God. If God dwells in your heart, you will be rooted and grounded in love.

Ephesians 3:17, "That Christ may dwell in your hearts by faith; that ye, being rooted and grounded in love."

Our love for God and people guarantees total victory in every area and makes us unbeatable and more than conquerors over any circumstance.

Romans 8:37 says, "Nay, in all these things we are more than conquerors through him that loved us."

Your love for God and His people is a threat to forces of darkness. Love will energize faith thereby making you a threat to the kingdom of darkness. Satan is aware that if you purpose in your heart to walk in faith and love, there is nothing he can do to stop you from receiving from God.

Your love in addition to your faith will conquer the adversary everywhere, anywhere, any day, anytime. When you walk in love, you indirectly program yourself for the redemptive blessing which makes your life resistible to sickness and poverty. Jesus summaries the laws with a single command: love God and your neighbour. This is a commandment for every believer to obey.

Matthew 22:37, "Jesus said unto him, Thou shalt love the Lord thy God with all thy heart, and with all thy soul, and with all thy mind. This is the greatest and the most important commandment. The second most important commandment is like it: 'Love your neighbor as you love yourself.'"

Strife, on the other hand, is deadly and evil, and can put your life on hold. Strife can stop the grace of God in your life. Confusion, being the twin brother of strife, will set in; likewise, evil things will begin to manifest. This is described in James 3:16: *"For where envying and strife is, there is confusion and every evil work."*

The Bible warns us again and again about the danger and consequences of strife and bitterness, either in the church, family, or work place. It is an evil instrument in the hand of the devil to diminish and stop believers from becoming increasingly prominent.

Strife is a common problem among many folks today. Knowingly and unknowingly, willingly and unwillingly, we allow it creep into our lives and our relationships, thereby stealing our peace and joy, and damaging our relationships.

The Bible admonishes us to stop strife before it causes any damage. Proverbs 17:14 (AMP), ***"The beginning of strife is as when water first trickles [from a crack in a dam]; therefore, stop contention before it becomes worse and quarrelling breaks out."***

Contention and bitterness will short-circuit your faith and make you stranded, confuses, and unfruitful in the things of God. Rather than meddling with strife, make up your mind to stand against it using the word of God whenever it shows up.

Strife affects you physically, spiritually, and emotionally. This was my experience when I had contentions with some of my co-pastors, 'labourers in the vineyard'. As a result of how much it affected my body and mind, I made a vow - until I see Jesus in glory - not to be involved in strife and bitterness anymore.

Everyone is not going to be nice to you on our Christian pilgrimage. There are people who are going to annoy and provoke you to anger; never allow them steal your peace, which is your source of health and life, but overcome the temptation to retaliate when you are tempted to.

Let us handle strife and offense like Jesus Christ did in the Bible. Matthew 5:38-39: ***"Ye have heard that it hath been said, An eye for an eye, and a tooth for a tooth: But I say unto you, that ye resist not evil: but whosoever shall smite thee on thy right cheek, turn to him the other also."***

No one could touch Jesus Christ when He went back to Nazareth. The religious leaders were angry at Him. They wanted to push him down from a cliff and even stone Him. But He never retaliated; rather, He walked away and they couldn't touch Him because He demonstrated the love of God towards those who hated Him.

"So Funke, what are you saying? If anyone slaps me on my right cheek, I should offer my left cheek? Until he/she kills me and send me to an untimely grave?"

No! That is not what I am saying. When Jesus said to turn the other cheek, He didn't mean for you to stand there to be killed. The law of retaliation or personal revenge was not intended or encouraged; rather, we are to be motivated by love at all times and believe that it will protect you from the attacks of your enemies. Love conquers, delivers, saves, protects, and heals all wounds. Love never fails.

I decided to write this book as a result of my ordeals and experiences with brethren of the faith whom I loved, who later turned their backs on and betrayed me. I felt nearly overcome by betrayal, anger, bitterness, and resentment. I was in a state of extreme turmoil. People I called my trusted friends and close confidants, people in whom I invested so much energy, time, and resources, had betrayed me.

Strife may not affect you negatively if it doesn't come from closely related persons. But when those involved are people you trust, love, cherish, and respect - such as pastors, friends, best friends, or close relatives - it can be quite painful.

Dear friend, make up your mind to leave the elementary school of bitterness, resentment, and anger and begin to walk in the love of God which makes you live the most powerful kind of life, a life without limit and reproach, a redemptive life without sickness and diseases.

CHAPTER ONE

God's Kind of Love:

A time is coming when unbelievers will naturally want to serve Jesus because of the love that radiates in our lives as His disciples. The Christian life is meant to be a mirror revealing and full of God's love, and there is need to demonstrate this love towards His people just as He demonstrated it towards us. For while we were yet sinners, Christ died for us. [Romans 5:8]

If you understand the love God has for mankind, you will not find it difficult to love others. This will not be an issue in your Christian race.

When I was in pain, so many thoughts passed through my mind. I thought God was my problem; maybe He wanted to kill me, didn't want me anymore. This was until I began to study about the love of God from His word and anointed messages of reputable men of God, where I discovered a revelation of God's unconditional love.

God is not witch; neither is He wicked. When you are in pain God wants to heal you, when you are broke He wants to bless you, when you are depressed God wants to encourage you, when you are oppressed He wants to deliver you.

When my breast pain was intense, I had forgotten how God loved me, how He delighted in my well-being, how He wanted me to have everything in abundance, and how He wanted me to be healed of my pain and move on with the work He has commissioned me to do.

I had heard for so long that whenever you occasionally and unintentionally fall into sin, God will just cut off your neck or strike you with sickness and disease, after which He will take you home; this meant you had finished your assignment on earth. I was walking in condemnation for so long and listening to the lies of the devil all day long. The Lord made provision for forgiveness (1John 1:9).

But I discovered His amazing love for me was revealed through the shedding of His blood on my behalf. I discovered His mercy was sufficient for mankind. I began to fill my mind with His love towards me. In doing that, the fear of death began to leave me.

Ephesians 2:4, *"But God, who is rich in mercy, for his great love wherewith he loved us."*

The nature of Jesus is love, and the same nature has been embedded into our spirit being. This gives us eternal life and enables us to demonstrate the God-kind-of-love to mankind.

Jesus told us plainly that the easiest way to identify His followers is through the nature of love His children exhibit; not through race, tribe, or church position. Being addicted to love is proof of our salvation.

1 John 4:7-8, *"Beloved, let us love one another: for love is of God, and every one that loveth is born of God, and knoweth God. He that loveth not knoweth not God; for God is love."*

In my accounting profession, there are test ratio analyses for determining the strengths and weaknesses of a firm. The financial advisor or accountant will evaluate various aspects of a company's operating and financial performance, such as its efficiency, liquidity, profitability, and solvency. He must use some key ratios to evaluate the performance and financial health of a company, and by doing that he can determine how viable a company is now and in five years to come.

In the same manner, the proof of being born again is our love affair with God and for His people. Love is the litmus test and the proof of our union with the Father. Let's look at these two scriptures.

John 13:34-35, *"A new commandment I give unto you, that ye love one another; as I have loved you, that ye also love one another. By this shall all men know that ye are my disciples if ye have love one to another."*

1 John 4:7-8 *"Beloved, let us love one another: for love is of God; and every one that loveth is born of God, and knoweth God. He that loveth not knoweth not God; for God is love."*

Jesus didn't live a life of selfish interest. He lived a perfect life of doing the will of His Father, offering Himself to serve, and helping everyone around Him. We need to realize that we no more carry the nature of the devil anymore, which is the selfish and destructive Adamic nature. We have now, in His infinite mercy, been translated from the power of darkness into the kingdom of His dear Son, and He has changed our state.

Love has made us pass from death to life. [Colossians 1:13] He has changed our unregenerated nature and given us a regenerated one.

John 3:14-15, *"We know that we have passed from death unto life because we love the brethren. He that loveth not his brother abideth in death. Whosoever hateth his brother is a murderer: and ye know that no murderer hath eternal life abiding in him."*

Emphatically, God is love. If God is love, we should try to understand what His love is all about. If we have been given a new life and nature that has the capacity to love like Christ does, then love is very important to our walk with God and doing His will. It is evidence of our justification and regeneration.

In 1 Corinthians 13, which is the New Testament psalm of love, love is described as charity, which is *agape* in the Greek word, the highest form of love; an important gift of the spirit that is more superior to all gifts. God's kind of love is the love that Jesus expressed to us during His lifetime.

Every believer must endeavour to understand the mysteries and forces of love and soberly reflect on the verses in 1 Corinthians 13:1-3. When you are endowed with all the gifts of the Holy Spirit and have no *agape* love (God's kind of love) it will profit you nothing; your faith will shrink, you will move no mountain.

Love is the driving force that fuels our faith. Without love, your giving is useless, tongues and prophecies are nothing and unfruitful. Answered prayers are almost impossible when you step out of love and refuse to forgive your brothers. No love, no faith; no faith, no blessing.

1 John 4:11-12, ***"Beloved, if God so loved us, we ought also to love one another. No man hath seen God at any time. If we love one another, God dwelleth in us, and his love is perfected in us."***

John 3:16 ***also states, "For God so loved the world, that he gave his only begotten Son, that whosoever believeth in him should not perish, but have everlasting life."***

How is your love for others? How far are you willing to go for another? Let us emulate and practice the love of the old believers, such as when Peter was in prison, the whole church prayed day and night without ceasing for him to be out.

Acts 12:5 ***"Peter, therefore, was kept in prison: but prayer was made without ceasing of the church unto God for him".***

Believers of today might say "It is the sin of the brother that landed him in trouble." "Let him die in prison." They might also be like Job's friends who posed a theory about his troubles when all hell broke loose against him.

We are called and equipped to demonstrate unflinching love towards one another against all odds. We must always be there to help during times of need and trouble. We are creatures of love, and through the Holy Spirit who abides in you, causing you to live a love-filled life, God has recreated you to be like Him.

GOD'S KIND OF UNITY
There is true and false unity. Examples of false unity include armed robbers coming together to do evil, a husband and wife choosing together to

lie (like Ananias and Sapphira did in the book of the Acts of the Apostles), children plotting with each other to defraud their parents, a group plotting against a pastor in a church or a political leader in the country.

There are also individuals uniting together to betray or kill another (like Herod and Pilate joining hands to kill our Lord Jesus (Luke 23:12) and the men, numbering over forty, who took an oath to kill Apostle Paul (Acts 23:12).

But true unity, the God kind of unity, is for truth, peace, holiness, and single-mindedness. A unified church or family is one that comes together in affection and determination to do good to all men, affect lives positively by having genuine concern and care for the well-being of the brethren, promoting the growth and development of the unified body. This is its common goal.

God wants all His children to live in harmony and in one accord with Christ Jesus.

Psalms 133:1, *"Behold, how good and how pleasant it is for brethren to dwell together in unity."*

Romans 15:5, *"Now the God of patience and consolation grant you to be likeminded one toward another according to Christ Jesus."*

Many believers have never seen themselves as one with other believers due to a lack of understanding of the spiritual truth of their adoption into one body through the Cross. Even when our Lord Jesus was about to be betrayed, He specifically prayed for the oneness of the church of God and demanded the exhibition of perfect unity from the church.

Christ commanded all His children to be one because we have been joined together in the Spirit. We are born again into the same family of God and have been translated from our biological parenthood to a spiritual parenthood. All believers must operate and function as siblings. Until we see ourselves as one body and one Spirit, the struggle for love continues.

1 Corinthians 12:13 *"For by one Spirit are we all baptized into one body, whether we be Jews or Gentiles, whether we be bond or free; and have been all made to drink into one Spirit."*

Philippians 2:2; *"Fulfil ye my joy, that ye be*

likeminded, having the same love, being of one accord, of one mind."

1 Corinthians 6:17 *says, "But he that is joined unto the Lord is one spirit."*

Malachi 2:10, *"Have we not all one father? Hath not one God created us? Why do we deal treacherously every man against his brother, by profaning the covenant of our fathers?"*

We must see ourselves as brethren; brothers and sisters, children of the same Father. This was the mentality I had when I gave my life to Jesus, back in school. In our fellowship on campus, we were so united as brethren and always ready to defend each other, especially those who were been unjustly treated by some ungodly lecturers.

We were ready to sacrifice our money (pocket money) for the Gospel and the well-being of student believers, just like the early church in the Bible. We were ready to return to fellowship with any of the brethren who were held back as a result of courses carried over. I was and am sown to Jesus. I love Jesus and His people with a passion.

When I have a job opening, I want to fill the position with God's people. I am always eager and looking for an opportunity to help people, more especially the people of God. When I became a Chartered Accountant, I obtained a recruiter's license from the government and used the opportunity to assist many, especially from the household of God.

Doing good to people became my hobby, giving without limit especially to God's people and the less privileged made me happy and fulfilled. I began to look for opportunities to make life better for people. I hate to see God's people suffer. I derive pleasure and satisfaction whenever I give a helping hand to the people of God. Love is a passion for me.

I remember, when I went into business that required professionals to handle, there was no better person to me than a fellow believer. Sadly, the privilege was abused and it turned out to be a mirage which gave birth to this book *'LOVE WITHOUT STRIFE.'*

Love (and unity) looks unto the interest of others before its own. Most importantly, as a believer, you are called to do good whenever you have the opportunity.

Galatians 6:10, *"As we have therefore opportunity, let us do good unto all men, especially unto them who are of the household of faith."*

Whenever I shut my eye against the people of God when I have the opportunity to do good, it takes my peace away immediately.

I remember helping a widow immensely in the area of rent bills and business empowerment twice. She consistently abused the opportunity by not handling her business well. The second time I rendered assistance to her, I gave her a warning to do well in business in order to be self-sufficient and not depend on anyone to pay her bills.

However, when the year ended, she came back again to solicit for business empowerment from my foundation. But, this time around, I had made up my mind not to help her again but teach her a lesson. After much pressure from her, I blocked her contact on my phone. After two weeks, I lost my peace. The Holy Spirit started dealing with me in that area of my action. I repented, unblocked her, and opened the channel of communication with her again, after which I rendered the assistance she requested.

Perfect love and unity have no limit. They require you to lay down your selfish desires in order to meet the needs of others. Our Lord Jesus laid down His life for us because He loves us. While you may not be able to lay down your life for anyone because Jesus has done that already, you can spare the time to intercede for those in need of prayers; for example, the sick.

When you choose to make an impact on the lives of those around you, you are being ruled by love and will surely leave a mark on your generation.

GOD'S KIND OF FORGIVENESS

Any believer who doesn't want to be out of fellowship with God should make forgiveness a top priority in his or her Christian life.

Forgiveness is not an option but a necessity. God has given His children the power to make a choice. You can either choose to forgive, and enjoy unlimited freedom and a happy, healthy life or hold grudges forever and end up stranded, miserable, unhappy, and unproductive.

Forgiveness is the master key to unlocking the heavens for the miraculous. It is the key to the kingdom that constantly connects and unites you to the wisdom and power of God.

The sole ground for human forgiveness is the price paid by our Lord Jesus on the cross of Calvary. God's forgiveness is purely through faith in Christ Jesus, not a result of our righteousness or good work. If God Himself could sacrifice such a gift to eliminate and blot out our sins, we are equally admonished to offer total forgiveness, not partial, to those who offend us and follow peace with them.

In the whole book of Philemon, Apostle Paul demonstrated the hallmark of a true leader, like our Lord Jesus, when he was writing a personal appeal letter to Philemon, a wealthy Christian slave owner.

Onesimus was converted during his ministerial journey and desired genuine Christian forgiveness and reconciliation with Philemon. Paul appealed to Philemon. He did not use his authority over him as a spiritual father. He told him to receive Onesimus forever not as a slave who stole from him, but as a beloved brother who was once unprofitable but now profitable to both of them in the ministry.

Paul further appealed to Philemon to charge any debt Onesimus owed against him to his [Paul's] account.

Philemon 1:17-19, *"If thou count me therefore a partner, receive him as myself. If he hath wronged thee, or oweth thee ought, put that on mine account; I Paul have written it with mine own hand, I will repay it: albeit I do not say to thee how thou owest unto me even thine own self besides."*

What manner of love! Incredible! What a leader worthy of emulation. This was just like what Jesus Christ did for us. He gave up His life so we could have ours back. He died so we could live like Him. All our debt and sin were charged to his account for us to be forgiven and He settled all our debt from His own account once and for all. Our record of sin was also destroyed completely.

Galatians 4:4-7, *"But when the proper time had fully come, God sent His Son, born of a woman, born subject to [the regulations of] the Law, to purchase the freedom of (to ransom, to redeem, to atone for) those who were subject to the Law, that we might be adopted and have sonship conferred upon us [and be recognized as God's sons]. And because you [really] are [His] sons, God has sent the [Holy] Spirit of His Son into our hearts, crying, Abba (Father)! Therefore, you are no longer a slave (bondservant) but a son; and if a son, then [it follows that you are] an heir by the aid of God, through Christ."* [AMP]

Isaiah 43:25, *"I, even I, am he that blotteth out thy transgressions for mine own sake, and will not remember thy sins."*

God's forgiveness doesn't see us as slaves anymore but as souls redeemed from sin and useful for the Kingdom. It doesn't remember old wounds. It is total because our sin is not imputed against us, neither remembered anymore.

You must forgive the way God forgives. He forgives totally, wholly, completely, and not partially. When you have an unforgiving nature, you are ruled by the flesh and cannot receive God's best for your life.

Ephesians 4:32, *"And be ye kind one to another, tender-hearted, forgiving one another, even as God for Christ's sake hath forgiven you."*

Every believer must possess a heart of total forgiveness and reconciliation with all men, if you want your Father in heaven to forgive you. Though you might have been hurt, rejected, and treated unfairly or even cruelly by others, which affected your emotional state, don't allow yourself to be held captive by anger, bitterness, and resentment or trapped by emotional bondage and self-pity.

I understand these feelings and have been there before. How did I break free? I allowed the power of forgiveness to set me free totally and make me whole again.

CHAPTER TWO

CHARACTERISTICS OF LOVE

Love is not a choice but a command from God. God views love seriously. Why? It is very important to our Christian journey and a determinant of many things in the kingdom. Love defines our level of relationship or association with God. Are you a friend of God?

The first covenant was made for the natural man. It was an outward circumcision. The products of this covenant could not demonstrate the true love of God. The new covenant came with a new commandment,

John 15:12-15 *" This is my commandment, That ye love one another, as I have loved you. Greater love hath no man than this, that a man lay down his life for his friends. Ye are my friends, if ye do whatsoever I command you. Henceforth I call you not servants; for the servant knoweth not what his lord doeth: but I have called you friends; for all things that I have heard of my Father I have made known unto you."*

John 13:34-35, *A new commandment I give unto you, That ye love one another; as I have loved you, that ye also love one another. By this shall all men know that ye are my disciples, if ye have love one to another.*

Jesus said that the degree of disciples' love for one another will determine the level of His intimacy with them. He stated that through the demonstration of their deeds of love for one another, the world will recognize and be convinced that the disciples are truly His, not necessarily by their doctrines, miracles they perform, and even their love for the lost.

Sometimes, we would like to show our outward love to unbelievers. However, they want to see how much we love ourselves first. Charity, people say, begins at home. You cannot give what you do not have. The question is, do we love ourselves in the kingdom today?

In 1 Corinthians 13, Apostle Paul describes this new kind of love, *agape*, as a love that is based on the deliberate choice of the one who loves rather than the worthiness of the one who is loved. This kind of love makes no sense to the natural man. It is giving, selfless, and expecting nothing in return.

Let's look at some of the significant characteristics of this kind of new love described in 1 Corinthians 13:4-8.

"Love suffers long and is kind; love does not envy; love does not parade itself, is not puffed up; does not behave rudely, does not seek its own, is not provoked, thinks no evil; does not rejoice in iniquity, but rejoices in the truth; bears all things, believes all things, hopes all things, endures all things. Love never fails. But whether there are prophecies, they will fail; whether there are tongues, they will cease; whether there is knowledge, it will vanish away."

LOVE DOES NOT WORK AGAINST HIS NEIGHBOUR'S WELLNESS

Romans 13:10, *"Love worketh no ill to his neighbour: therefore, love is the fulfilling of the law."*

The God kind of love neither mistreats nor harm people. It doesn't work against the progress of others. You must learn how to treat other people well and not hold grudges against any.

LOVE ALWAYS BELIEVES THE BEST

Love always believes the best of the people. During my ordeal, when I was cheated, mistreated, and my love was equally betrayed by the people I loved, I began to resent pastors. I didn't want to trust any pastor anymore, not even the Pope or General Overseer of any kind. I started criticizing and judging them, and made up my mind not to have anything to do with them anymore.

I concluded they were responsible for my depression, discouragement, emotional pain, bodily pain, and the alarming symptoms in my body which I had never experienced before now. *"Oh, I would soon die"* was the thought that was coming to me. I perceived death and believed they would contribute to my early grave and yet these people would attend my funeral and say nonsense tributes. Those were the thoughts that the devil programmed in my mind during that period.

The enemy really pushed me to criticize, condemn, and judge them because they caused so much harm to my body and my family. But when I started believing God for bodily and emotional healing, judging and criticizing was one of those things I needed to repent from. I needed to receive forgiveness for my own negative actions and resentments.

I stopped discussing the issues with anybody and, instead, started spending about thirty minutes each day praying for them.

When you are walking in the light of the word of God, love will choose to believe and treat people who offended you with mercy and forgiveness, even though they might have critically harmed you. Never retaliate against the shortcomings of others. Also, it is not our job as believers to judge others.

Romans 14:4, *"Who are you to judge another's servant? To his own master he stands or falls. Indeed, he will be made to stand, for God is able to make him stand."*

God doesn't want us to judge another believer. It is to our own advantage to withhold judgment from them so that you yourself will not be judged.

According to Matthew 7:1-to, *"Judge not, that you be not judged. For with what judgment you judge, you will be judged; and with the measure you use, it will be measured back to you."*

There were several occasions where I had the opportunity again to judge these believers. The devil would occasionally remind me of past sagas. But I would always resist the devil. "Away from my side; they are forgiven and I have forgotten about it." Don't give the devil any place because he will always bring situations to your memory in a bid to form negative thinking patterns. Always resist him and he will flee.

LOVE IS SACRIFICIAL

God's kind of love is not selfish, but caring enough to offer a sacrifice even when it is not convenient.

John 3:16, *"For God so loved the world, that he gave his only begotten Son, that whosoever believeth in him should not perish, but have everlasting life."*

God's love seeks to go the extra mile to satisfy humanity. He sends rain on everyone, both the just and the unjust, and loves both the lovable and the unlovable. We were loved by Him even when we were sinners. [Romans 5:8] Whether or not we choose to respond and accept that love, He still loves us.

Like God, your attitude should be to continue to love, whether you are loved or not. This sacrificial love is one you demonstrate when no one loves you back. It is unselfish and sacrifices itself for the benefit of others.

Unless we are born of God, we will not be able to demonstrate this God-kind of love because it comes with the new nature which is your new being. You must be ready to treat those who hurt or mistreat you kindly and refuse to be resentful, treat them wrongly, or retaliate even when you have the power to do so. That is meekness.

There is great reward from the Father when you do good to people and love your enemies.

Luke 6:35-36, *"But love ye your enemies, and do good, and lend, hoping for nothing again; and your reward shall be great, and ye shall be the children of the Highest: for he is kind unto the unthankful and to the evil. Be ye therefore merciful, as your Father also is merciful."*

God wants us to love our enemies, how much more God's people when they err. Be merciful unto those who hurt or defraud you. This is what God would desire.

LOVE RESTRAINS FROM DOING EVIL

When the love of God is engrafted into your nature and gains control over your spirit, it will always take possession of your thinking, behaviour, and actions, and always constrain and hold you back from wrongdoing. However, it is sad to see so many of today's believers not only doing evil but equally rendering evil with evil.

Joseph demonstrated the God kind of love towards his brethren when he had opportunity to retaliate. He would have used his exalted position to deal with his brothers, rather he showed them love and mercy and put them in the best land at Goshen. (Genesis 47)

Apostle Paul gave a sound warning stating that no one is permitted to render evil for evil but should, instead, always pursue what is good, both to yourself and to others. (1 Thessalonians 5:15)

True love disciplines self to let go of any ungodly lifestyle. True love doesn't take advantage of an employer to enrich his pocket. You must not use your position in the ministries (secular) or private companies to enrich your pocket through corruption. As a Christian, you are a sanctified vessel, called to live righteously unto God. You are God's ambassador; therefore, iniquity and evil shouldn't be found in your heart.

Matthew 5:7, ***"Blessed are the merciful: for they shall obtain mercy."***

Jesus loved people and was moved with compassion to heal the sick, feed the five thousand, deliver many. He was challenged by the suffering of humanity.

Selfishness is a wicked robber which comes to steal good relationships. It ruins happy homes and wrecks the church of God. If not tamed on time, it will lead to hatred, jealousy, and murder. Our love must be without selfishness which leads to or breeds hypocrisy.

Agape, or Jesus' kind of love, never gives room to jealousy, bitterness, hatred, or murder. Love will never say, "If I cannot have it, let it not succeed." Instead, it says, "He is my brother, she is my sister. I don't want to hurt him or her. That project or business must succeed."

Love solves problems; it does not aggravate issues. Love will not embarrass his brother or sister in the court or any legal dispute-settling institute in order to show off. To live in the love of God is to admit our own mistakes, to end strife, to end quarreling, to forgive, to get rid of bitterness, hatred, and live in harmony with one another.

In an African setting such as in Nigeria, in the olden days, when you are called to serve in an exalted position, your family will call you and warn you to remember the son of whom you are. The whole family would gather together to appeal to you not to bring shame on or tarnish the image of the family name.

However, today the story is different. When a man is given an appointment to serve in the government, his family and kinsmen will organize a rousing party for him and tell him "This is our turn, our chance, our quota; an opportunity which comes but once." They believe their own God is a God of opportunities and that position is one such opportunity, provided to amass wealth to themselves rather than transform and serve the masses. A shame on such individuals and leaders!

1 Thessalonians 5:22, *"Abstain from all appearance of evil."*

2 Timothy 2:19, *Nevertheless the foundation of God standeth sure, having this seal, The Lord knoweth them that are his. And, let every one that nameth the name of Christ depart from iniquity."*

As a Christian, you are not permitted to do what others are doing. When others are falsifying records to make money, you don't want to participate. When others are defrauding their employers, you are singled out of the mess.

I have served in two government parastatals in Abuja, Nigeria. Before I resigned my appointment as an auditor of a very good government parastatal, my colleagues looked at me as a *blocker*, someone who didn't need any money. If the love of God was absent in my life, I would have joined the multitude to ruin or defraud my employer. Making money was very easy for me; all files, including disbursements, passed through my table. but it would have led me to hellfire.

True love is righteous and shuns evil all the time. Many times, the love of God constrained me from writing false reports or collecting bribes over a wrong file. There were many things happening that displeased me as a believer and equally displeased my maker.

When I realized my future and destiny as a pastor was in danger, I decided to quit because I wanted to please God. I prayed about it and God led me to resign my appointment. This I have never regretted to this day. I set up my own private company and God blessed the work of my hands.

In the same vein, the love of God also constrained Joseph not to defile his body when he had the opportunity to do so with Potiphar's wife. (Genesis 37:7-13) Joseph called that act "wickedness against God". When you sin against God, it is an act of wickedness. Each time you remember your love towards God, you don't want to do things the way others do them. Love wants to please the Maker at all times.

LOVE DOESN'T REJOICE IN EVIL OR THE INIQUITY OF OTHERS

According to Proverbs 24:16-18, *"For a just man falleth seven times, and riseth up again: but the wicked shall fall into mischief. Rejoice not when thine enemy falleth, and let not thine heart be glad when he stumbleth. Lest the LORD see it, and it displease him, and he turn away his wrath from him."*

1 Corinthians 13:6, *"Rejoiceth not in iniquity, but rejoiceth in the truth."*

As God's children, we must not glory or rejoice over anyone's misfortune. If we are walking in love, we are not permitted to smile when others are going through challenges, torments, or trouble at any time. Even when our enemies are failing, we do not rejoice. Love keeps us from celebrating evil.

When the brethren are in trouble, it is our call to pray. Love bears people's burdens. It says, "Your problem is my problem, your victory is my victory, your trials and battles are mine, your pains are my pains." This was the way I was brought up when I gave my life to Christ.

In the students' fellowship back on campus, we were united in such a way that if anything happened to any of our members, we were ready to stand by him or her; physically and spiritually. The Bible records that when Peter was in prison, the brethren prayed without ceasing for his release. (See Acts 12:5)

Sad to say, we don't find such love in the church again today. We are sometimes surrounded by selfish people, who love you because of what they get from you. These are also in our workplaces; (contractors' love) who only love a position rather than the person, the gifts rather than the giver. They love you because of your juicy position which is tied to contracts they seek to be beneficiaries of. However, once your tenure expires, the love expires too!

I remember some years back one of my senior pastors was having a challenge in his office. His boss was bent on removing him from his position. We shared the pain and suffering together. I made it mandatory to leave my office every week to visit, encourage, and pray with him in the office.

During this period, we acted according to Acts 12:5. ***"Peter therefore was kept in prison: but prayer was made without ceasing of the church unto God for him".*** My husband was the head of the prayer team in our local church at the time. With four other close family friends, we came together and had a seven-day vigil for our pastor, praying for divine intervention. To the glory of God, the head of the secular ministry made a great mistake and was dismissed from the office and our pastor was vindicated! God answers prayers when we walk in love.

I remember one of our church members who was posted outside the country as an Ambassador. He was denied the promotion in his office. Because of his eye challenges, he was denied the opportunity of writing the promotional examination with a magnifying computer machine.

One day, he called me and told me the story, asking if there was any help I could render. He put up a protest letter and sent it to me, and I did the necessary follow up on his behalf at the Civil Service Commission. To cut a long story short, he was called upon to write the exams which he passed; and to the glory of God, his promotion letter was backdated and salary arrears paid to him. He later retired honourably on the desired grade. Love fights for others.

LOVE DOESN'T ENVY OTHERS

If our love is not self-seeking but directed towards others, we will rejoice in the blessings they receive rather than desiring those blessings for ourselves. People whose minds are preoccupied with selfish love can be disturbed and feel uncomfortable when other fellows are making progress or succeeding.

Agape love has no room for jealousy. Envy is an enemy of love. It is a spirit and one of the works of the flesh listed in Romans 1:29. ***"Being filled with all unrighteousness, fornication, wickedness, covetousness, maliciousness; full of envy, murder, debate, deceit, malignity; whisperers."***

Envy is an evil thought which originates from our mind; it is a very serious sin that must not be allowed to have a foothold in our lives. A very delicate issue, it can lead to murder if unchecked.

There are lots of stories about pastors who are envious of pastors of other churches with large populations. Some of them try to seek satanic powers and anointing, not patient with God. They enter covenants with the devil. Within a short period, they start having big buildings, big churches, and huge crowds. They ride in expensive cars and live in expensive apartments. I learnt one such pastor lost his three children within a year. He was fed up and wanted to quit the pact he had made but was told it was too late. He lost his life. Envy!

I also remember some time ago, a man who told our senior pastor who was intervening in the issue concerning my project, "Let them write it down, I will make sure that the project will not succeed. I am coming out with another joker." Envy and jealousy were behind that statement. But the book of Lamentations 3:37 says, *"Who is he that saith and it cometh to pass, when the Lord commandeth it not?"* Today, the project has succeeded.

Love does not speak that way. Love rejoices with those who are rejoicing and prays for other people's progress. It will not speak arrogantly but, rather, wants to see others succeed. Envious thoughts must be resisted continually; never give room to the flesh. Most of the murder committed in homes, offices, schools, and even churches start from envy.

Envy made Cain to kill Abel because of his offering which was acceptable in the sight of

God. Envy was the reason Saul wanted to kill David. Our Lord Jesus' ministry was envied by the Jewish leaders who handed him over for crucifixion.

Mark 15:10: *"For he knew that the chief priests had delivered him for envy."*

Romans 13:13-14, *"Let us walk honestly, as in the day; not in rioting and drunkenness, not in chambering and wantonness, not in strife and envying. But put ye on the Lord Jesus Christ, and make not provision for the flesh, to fulfil the lusts thereof."*

God wants us to walk honestly and in integrity with one another, not with strife, envy, or jealousy. Envy and jealousy will lead to malice and make you keep a distance from those succeeding. Never treat envy and jealousy with kid gloves. Both are enemies that can block your blessings and also affect your life.

Proverbs 14:30, *"A sound heart is the life of the flesh: but envy the rottenness of the bones."*

Guard your mind and refuse to process evil thoughts. Always renew your mind with the word of God. [Romans 12:1-2]

LOVE DOES NOT OWE

I am going to emphasize a little on this point because it is common among believers. The God-kind of love never takes pride or joy in owing any man. It is always eager to pay debts, either owed to the government or to individuals. It never looks for loopholes or opportunities to defraud or evade debt payments.

I have seen brethren eager to use the technicalities of the law to sue their landlords in order to evade rent payment. Even when the court rules in favour of the landlord, overnight they would vacate the property and rent another house without settling the outstanding rent or liabilities. Such people leave with a curse and sin hanging on their necks which will one day manifest.

Many believers today are owing here and there, even from the church purse, with no intention of paying back; even when they have the opportunity to.

Romans 13:8 says, *"Owe no man anything, but to love one another: for he that loveth another hath fulfilled the law."*

Romans 13:8 NIV, *"Let no debt remain outstanding, except the continuing debt to love one another, for whoever loves others has fulfilled the law."*

When your rent is due for payment or you are owing either unbelievers or your fellow believers, pay them. When you are owing your tithe or what you borrowed from the church purse, please pay it. Without that, you are sinning against God and the people you are owing. Some believers are been stagnated or stranded because of violating that commandment.

Let me tell you a story. A Muslim staff of my organization who hailed from the northern part of Nigeria died a few years back. When our company wanted to pay his entitlements, I was made to realize by his religious colleague that the debt he was owing needed to be settled first, while the remaining balance should be paid to the family. Without his debt being settled, the guy in question will not enter Heaven according to the Islamic faith.

Well, it is the same in Christianity. The difference is there is no repentance or room to make amends after death. The Bible says in Hebrews 9:27, *"And as it is appointed for men to die once, but after this the judgment."* All debts have to be paid before you leave the earth.

Let us desist from this sinful habit of owing which can block your blessings and eventually lead you to hell fire. The only obligation and debt you owe God and His people is love.

Over seventy percent of my company's debtors today are believers; even some are pastors. Although I am quite aware of their financial status, however, they unfortunately do not want to pay. Anyone who takes pleasure in owing others the scriptures consider such a one a wicked person.

Psalms 37:21, ***"The wicked borrows and does not repay, But the righteous shows mercy and gives."***

Agape love doesn't owe anyone anything but love. It gives and shows mercy.

If you love your friends or family and want their businesses to succeed, stop owing them. Everybody knows the effect of bad and doubtful debt on a company.

Nothing liquidates, kills, or collapses businesses like debt. If any company runs down or folds up as result of debtors' liability and you are one of them, God considers you a wicked person. You contributed to the downfall of others and He will hold you accountable on the last day. Believers, please repent and desist from this sinful act.

LOVE DOES NOT SEEK ITS OWN

Agape love is true. It's not selfish and never intends to seek its own. Some people love and always feel concerned and passionate about themselves. But true love lives for others. It always has concerns about the welfare of others; especially the beloved.

To receive love, you must be resolute to give love. You cannot give what you do not have. To be loved is to love others. Our love must be without selfishness. Selfishness is a wicked robber that leads to or breeds hypocrisy. It comes to steal good relationships, ruins happy homes, and wrecks the church of God. If not tamed on time, it will lead to envy, hatred, and even murder.

Galatians 6:2, ***"Bear ye one another's burdens, and so fulfil the law of Christ."***

LOVE IS FEARLESS

The agape kind of love is not fearful but bold with no anxiety. The Bible says, ***"There is no fear in love; but perfect love casteth out fear: because fear hath torment. He that feareth is not made perfect in love."*** 1 John 4:18

LOVE IS KIND

True love always wants to share in your pain and your joy. It has compassion and a caring heart towards humanity. Love thinks about other people's feelings and renders acts of benevolence to others even when it is not convenient.

LOVE SUFFERS FOR A LONG TIME

Love is patient and persistent. It doesn't give up on people but stays believing the best can come of them, just as God does with you. This kind of love that Apostle Paul inspires us to have is contrary to the world's intellectual reasoning that encourages us to avoid people who are perceived to be difficult to get along with, whether they are friends or family members.

True love is patient with the imperfection of others and ready to give what it takes. Never retaliate at the shortcomings of others. Perfect love knows no boundary and is resolute. Love is lifetime commitment. Love should be our motivating factor in doing things. True love will indeed promote peace and unity; not only in our homes but in the church.

LOVE AND THE HOME

Love makes a home. It adds value to our home. Love makes it beautiful. There is a difference between a home and a house. A home is spiritual while a house is physical. A house can be designed and built by a civil engineer. Due to the spiritual structure of a home, it can only be designed and built by God.

The first home created by God for Adam and Eve was an ideal home, full of joy. It was heaven on earth. It was spiritual. It was a replica of the kingdom of God on earth. They lived and enjoyed the higher life. It was the first house fellowship and a micro church. God was a member of the house fellowship. It was full of God's light and glory and a wonderful home, created by and radiating the love of God.

Love is spiritual and a creative force. It creates a home and makes it beautiful. As the flowers cover naked areas of the soil and make it beautiful, so love covers the rough spots in humanity. It is love and only love that gives us a sacred place called home.

When love comes and dwells in a home, it makes it a blissful and joyful place. Where there is no love, there is no home. All you may find is a house, irrespective of its creativity, the design of the building, or how expensive the furniture and landscaping may be.

A home may, therefore ,be defined as a place where a man and woman who have received eternal life dwell together in harmony. Where polygamous marriage is practiced, they have no home. It is just a habitation.

Love is the greatest thing in the world. When love is dead, life has lost its values. When we walk out of love, we walk out of the will of God. Love is the reason for life.

CHAPTER THREE

POWER IN LOVE AND UNITY

U nity is the strength of any church or family, and there is nothing compared to unity that can bring blessings to God's people or the individual. Unity is priceless, precious, and a rare commodity.

David, the author of the Psalms, dedicated a whole chapter to unity -in Psalms 133, he states:
"How good and how pleasant it is for brethren to dwell together in unity. It is like the precious ointment upon the head that ran down the beard; even Aaron's beard: that went down to the skirts of his garment; As the dew of Hermon, and as the dew that descended upon the mountains of Zion: for there the Lord commanded the blessing even life for evermore." (verses 1-3)

There is a need for people to live together in peace and harmony. David himself said living in unity is like holy anointing oil upon a man's head, and the dew of Hermon, which falls on the mountain of Zion.

David also made us understand in verse 3 of the same chapter, that unity is an idea of God poured out upon His people. Paul equally admonished and appealed to us to be of the same mind and maintain the unity of the spirit in the bond of peace.

1 Corinthians 1:10: *"But God hath revealed them unto us by his Spirit, for the Spirit searcheth all things, yea, the deep things of God."*

Philippians 2:1-3: *"If there be therefore any consolation in Christ, if any comfort of love, if any fellowship of the Spirit, if any bowels and mercies, fulfill ye my joy, that ye be likeminded, having the same love, being of one accord, of one mind, let nothing be done through strife or vainglory, but in lowliness of mind, let each esteem other better than themselves".*

Ephesians 4:3: *"Endeavouring to keep the unity of the spirit in the bond of peace, We must see ourselves as brethren born from the same womb".*

Galatians 3:28: *"There is neither Jew nor Greek, there is neither bond nor free, there is neither male nor female. for ye are all one in Christ Jesus."*

The psalmist declared to us that dwelling in unity is absolutely good and pleasing to God and mankind. God is vehemently against hatred and disunity. Satan understood this fact from the beginning, so he embarks on a mission to bring dissension and conflict among brethren and families. Right from creation, he sowed the seed of confusion in the lives of Adam and Eve and tricked them into believing his lies.

Practically speaking, every believer desires to please God. Disagreement, however, is one of the chief devices used by the devil to destroy the Gospel and the families of God's people. Unity will break the backbone of the devil, and families and the society as a whole will experience tremendous progress when they are united. We will flow better in spirit and in other areas if we are in unity.

This is so important. The church and the family that dwell together will see the blessings and glory of God. Unity is a very powerful weapon against the enemy.

In the New Testament, Paul made an appeal again to all the brethren not to be divided.

1 Corinthians 1:10-14 ESV: *"I appeal to you, brothers, by the name of our Lord Jesus Christ, that all of you agree, and that there be no divisions*

among you, but that you be united in the same mind and the same judgment. For it has been reported to me by Chloe's people that there is quarrelling among you, my brothers. What I mean is that each one of you says - "I follow Paul," or "I follow Apollos," or "I follow Cephas," or "I follow Christ". Is Christ divided? Was Paul crucified for you? Or were you baptized in the name of Paul? I thank God that I baptized none of you except Crispus and Gaius."

1 Peter 3:8-9 *[BBE Translation]: "Last of all, see that you are all in agreement, feeling for one another, loving one another like brothers, full of pity, without pride. Not giving back evil for evil, or curse for curse, but in place of cursing, blessing; because this is the purpose of God for you that you may have a heritage of blessing."*

In the scriptures above, Apostle Paul categorically appeals to believers about four major characteristics every Christian should have.

1. To be of one mind: Though this, to the natural mind, may not look feasible to humans, yet God wants us to always be exactly of the same mind, like-minded, love, and have a common voice.

In Romans chapter 12, the Bible admonishes us to renew our mind with the word of God, and through the word, our mind will fall in line with the Spirit of God. For with God nothing shall be impossible.

Let us examine the story of Babel in Genesis 11:1-9, where the people were united and determined in their hearts to succeed. The whole earth was of one language and the descendants of Noah, united by the strong bond of a common language, decided to build a tower whose top may reach unto heaven. "

The design was practically achievable and could be executed, because of unity. But God Himself came down and destroyed their plans by confounding their language.

Genesis 11:6: *"And the Lord said, behold the people is one and they have all one language and this they begin to do and now nothing will be restrained from them which they have imaged to do."*

God wants a united church and family. Gossips and mongers create strife. Whenever there is disagreement and division among members of the church, it will crumble and rupture the growth of the church. Satan and his agents cannot defeat or destroy a united family or a united church. Not even God Himself, because God cannot do evil.

Amos 3:3 says: *"Can two walk together except they agree?"*

Ecclesiastes 4:9 says: *"Two are better than one."*

God and man cannot walk together except man agrees with God and His word, because where there is no friendship, there can be no fellowship. Walking in agreement with one another and with God will take you far in the journey of life.

Romans 15:5-6,: *"Now the God of patience and consolation grant you to be likeminded one toward another according to Christ Jesus: That ye may with one mind and one mouth glorify God, even the Father of our Lord Jesus Christ."*

Romans 12:16: *"Be of the same mind one toward another...condescend to men of low estate."*

Philippians 2:2: *"Be likeminded, having the same love, being of one accord, of one mind."*
(See also Acts 2:46; Philippians 4:2)

2. To have compassion for one another: Some believers are wounded in their spirit. some are battered and shattered, while some are in pain. Apostle Paul urged believers to show compassion to one another, by acknowledging and identifying with the pain and suffering of their brethren, and desire to do something about it.

By showing compassion, it will be easier to forgive when we are wronged.

Ephesians 4:32: *"And be ye kind one to another, tender-hearted, forgiving one another, even as God for Christ's sake hath forgiven you"*.

We have to emulate Jesus, perfect example, in showing compassion. He showed compassion to the sick, to the hungry, to the lost, and those who mourned when He was on this earth.

Matthew 9:36: *"But when he saw the multitudes, he was moved with compassion on them, because they fainted, and were scattered abroad, as sheep having no shepherd"*.

Being compassionate will restrain you from doing or being evil. Just like Jesus, you cannot close your eyes when you see a sinner perishing; instead, you should win his or her soul to Christ. You cannot see the poor going hungry or naked and not want to cloth them.

Make it a daily practice to show kindness and compassion to somebody out there.

Galatians 6:2: *"Bear ye one another's burdens, and so fulfil the law of Christ."*

3. **To love one another:** Apostle Paul teaches us to love our brethren. Love is not a choice but a command that every believer that desires to possess eternal life must practice and obey. Loving God and His people is the mark of a true disciple of Jesus Christ. People will see the evidence that you are born of God when you are in love.

John 13:34-35: *"A new commandment I give unto you, That ye love one another; as I have loved you, that ye also love one another. By this shall all men know that ye are my disciples, if ye have love one to another."*

There is power in love and unity. God is love. If you love God, you will naturally love his people.

In 1 John 4:7-8 the Bible says: *"My loved ones, let us have love for one another: because love is of God, and everyone who has love is a child of God and has knowledge of God. He who has no love has no knowledge of God, because God is love."*

Love is a sign of knowing God. If you don't love man, you can't love God. Love is the sum of righteousness and the test of our being born of God. Our sincere love for our brethren is what distinguishes us as followers of Christ, irrespective of colour, race, tribe, or culture.

1 John 4:21 (ESV): *"And this commandment we have from Him; whoever loves God also loves his brother."*

Paul admonished believers to bear with one another, submit to one another, speak to one another with Psalms and hymns, encourage one another daily, live in harmony with one another, be sympathetic with one another, accept one another just as Christ accepted us, love one another; not slander one another, not steal from one another, not lie against one another, or deceive one another.

To love one another is to love your fellow brothers and sisters as Christ loves us.

SOURCES OF DISUNITY

As good and as pleasant as unity and love are, both can easily be fractured, punctured, and destroyed. We grieve God whenever we are divisive and unloving towards each other.

There are various sources of disunity and I will quickly discuss some of them below.

Satan And His Agents

One of the major sources of disunity is strife. The devil specializes in causing strife and disunity in the human life. He is the architect of disunity and strife and the enemy of unity and love. Our Heavenly Father is the author of love and unity. The Bible says that every good and perfect gift comes from God (James 1:17).

You must not allow the devil to use you as an instrument to destroy unity in relationships. Satan has come to kill, steal, and destroy. He doesn't like a united family or church and is ready to do anything possible to thwart a good relationship. But glory be to God who has given us power over the unclean spirit. (Luke 9:1-2)

CARNALITY

Apostle Paul frowned and reproved the Corinthian Christians for their frequent contentions, which are true evidence of carnality. We cannot move higher in life if we continue to live a carnal life. Carnality is a product of an unrenewed mind. Paul expressed his displeasure at his inability to disseminate spiritual information to them because of their carnality.

1 Corinthians 3:1-3: *"And I, brethren, could not speak unto you as unto spiritual, but as unto carnal, even as unto babes in Christ. I have fed you with milk, and not with meat: for hitherto ye were not able to bear it, neither yet now are ye able. For ye are yet carnal: for whereas there is among you envying, and strife, and divisions, are ye not carnal, and walk as men?"*

The flesh is the greatest enemy of man. Paul warned that those who practice the work of the flesh will be shut out of heaven. To be successful in moving with God, we must set ourselves in earnest to mortify the deeds of the body and walk in the newness of life.

When you see believers walking in strife, variance, wrath, divisiveness, and anger, it means their salvation is questionable. If they are saved, they are not making the effort to subdue the flesh, our corrupt nature.

You cannot be born again and allow your growth to be stunted or retarded. This will cause you to operate in the flesh frequently.

Galatians 5:19-23: *"Now the works of the flesh are manifest, which are these: adultery, fornication, uncleanness, lasciviousness, Idolatry, witchcraft, hatred, variance, emulations, wrath, strife, seditions, heresies, envy, murder, drunkenness, revelling, and such like; of the which I tell you before, as I have also told you in time past, that they which do such things shall not inherit the kingdom of God, But the fruit of the Spirit is love, joy, peace, longsuffering, gentleness, goodness, faith, Meekness, temperance: against such there is no law."*

Our body is not designed to obey God or please Him, but our spirit is. The body essentially wants to promote the work of the flesh on a daily basis, which is why our major spiritual battle as believers is a battle against the flesh and the mind. The flesh is intolerant and always eager and ready to retaliate when offended, but you must be ready to subdue it if you want to please God.

Romans 8:8 [ESV] says: *"Those who are in the flesh cannot please God."*

The battle of the flesh is the battle you must win, because the devil will see to it that you perpetually live in the flesh in order not to please God. The works of the flesh are hurtful, both to man and his brethren.

In order not to give in to the flesh, Paul admonishes every believer to walk in the renewed or regenerated nature by putting on the fruit of the spirit.

Galatians 5:16-18 *"This I say then, Walk in the Spirit, and ye shall not fulfil the lust of the flesh. For the flesh lusteth against the Spirit, and the Spirit against the flesh: and these are contrary the one to the other, so that ye cannot do the things that ye would. But if ye be led of the Spirit, ye are not under the law."*

Real Christians must endeavour to embrace a life that pleases the master. Let us strive to avoid division and strife as we would avoid a plague.

These were the reasons Apostle Paul could not speak the deep things of God to the Corinthians.

1 Corinthians 2:14; *"But the natural man receiveth not the things of the Spirit of God: for they are foolishness unto him: neither can he know them, because they are spiritually discerned."*

Though you may have life in Christ, as long as you are weak in the spirit or ruled by a carnal nature, you are a babe in Christ. You will not be able to understand the secret things of God; even hearing the voice of the spirit will be difficult.

God wants His children to come out of babyhood and pampers Christianity and become perfect men, unto the measure of the stature of the fullness of Christ. Let every believer strengthen their inner mind in order to avoid contention, strife, anger, and bitterness which are destroyers of unity, love, and good relationships.

THE LOVE OF MONEY, GREED, AND JEALOUSY

This is another root cause of strife and disunity. Money is good. It widens the scope of your choice and answers all things, just as Ecclesiastes 10:19b says. However, as good as money is, love for it can destroy relationships in a minute. Many conflicts today are driven by the love of money and greed. 1 Timothy 6:10a: *"For the love of money is the root of all evil."*

The evil done because of money is enormous. Many couples have been torn apart because of financial issues and too many siblings fight and are split apart over family inheritances. Too many good relationships have been dissolved because of money. Many people have been betrayed, too many churches have packed up because of trustees fighting over money, many pastors have left pastoral jobs, and so many have left their place of abode because of money.

In my life, I have maintained good and solid relationships with people; but because of money and greed, two or three of those relationships dear to me were thwarted and crashed, because they wanted to take what belonged to me.

Judas had a good relationship with the Master until he betrayed Him because of greed. Love for money and greed can be harmful to a healthy relationship.

DECEPTION

You can't build a healthy relationship on deception. Deception by either party will harm a relationship. Jacob deceitfully got the family blessing which was rightfully meant for his brother, Esau, in accordance with tradition. His relationship with his brother was wrecked for twenty years!

Deception, scheming, and manipulation will wreck or cause havoc in any relationship, either among siblings, husband and wife, close friends, or business partners.

Humorously, Jacob was also a victim of deception in the house of Laban and ended up with a wife he did not really want to marry. He reaped what he sowed.

DISHONESTY

Any relationship built on honesty can be sustained for life. You are likely to keep a job with an honest mind. Employers are always looking for honest labourers/employees and individuals looking for an honest wife; and vice versa. Many businesses have folded up as a result of dishonesty among partners. Many homes are in ruins as a result of disloyalty. When one party is not sincere and has an affair outside the matrimonial home, such a union is heading for the rocks.

If you want a lasting relationship, honesty must be your watchword.

PRIDE

Pride is the forerunner of destruction. It is one of the major causes of disunity among couples, business partners, and other forms of relationships.

It destroys relationships easily. When a wife feels superior to her husband because of her financial or educational advantage over him, or vice versa, trouble looms.

Pride is a situation where one makes one looks down upon the other. God says He hates pride and would humble the proud. Pride is the forerunner to destruction [Proverbs 16:18].

James 4:6 says, *"But he giveth more grace. Wherefore he saith, God resisteth the proud, but giveth grace unto the humble."*

1 Peter 5:5: *"Likewise, ye younger, submit yourselves unto the elder. Yea, all of you be subject one to another, and be clothed with humility: for God resisteth the proud, and giveth grace to the humble."*

LACK OF PRAYER

The prayer of faith moves mountains, breaks satanic strongholds, and keeps enemies at bay. A prayerless Christian is a powerless Christian, and therefore vulnerable to satanic attacks because he lacks protective cover.

It is very easy for the devil to plant the evil seeds of disunity in a home that slumbers spiritually (Matthew 13:24,25)

LACK OF MUTUAL RESPECT FOR ONE ANOTHER

Every relationship, marriage, business, etc, must be based on mutual respect. Over-familiarity can lead to taking each other for granted. This has led to strife even in many Christian homes.

BENEFITS OF WALKING IN LOVE, UNITY, AND FORGIVENESS

It really pays and is beneficial to walk in harmony, love, and forgiveness. Walking in disunity, hatred, or unforgiveness hinders one's anointing. This is why the devil will see to it that you become bitter and resentful towards those who hurt you.

Walking in love, unity, and forgiveness is walking in power and dominion. You need to choose to forgive and walk in love again and again. If you don't, you will be the one who is going to suffer, not the people that hurt you. Some of the benefits of walking in love, unity, and forgiveness are:

Guaranteed Answers To Prayers

One of the major ways to receive answers to your prayers is walking in obedience to God's word and commandments. Bitterness, unforgiveness, and strife will block answers to prayers. You must obey the laws of love and forgiveness if you want to constantly receive from God.

Mark 11:24-26: *"Therefore I say unto you, what things soever ye desire, when ye pray, believe that ye receive them, and ye shall have them. And when ye stand praying, forgive, if ye have ought against any: that your Father also which is in heaven may forgive your trespasses. But if ye do not forgive, neither will your Father which is in heaven forgive your trespasses."*

Once your love is distorted, your faith stops working because faith works by love, and you need faith to receive from God. Forgive and stop discussing how you were mistreated, cheated, or wounded. You don't need to get mad at your offenders anymore. Don't lodge their offense in your heart; instead, release them totally now from your heart if you want God to show up quickly in your affairs.

That was what I did when I needed healing for my breast pain and the symptoms that came with it. I stopped talking about those who caused my pains, those who cheated me, and those who betrayed me with anyone, instead, I released them from my heart and started praying for them like never before.

Walking in love, unity, and forgiveness is the absolute key to blessings, deliverance, healing, and prosperity.

Inheritance Of Blessings From Above
God Himself promised to command blessings upon those who dwell in unity.

Psalms 133:1-3: *"Behold, how good and how pleasant it is for brethren to dwell together in unity! It is like the precious ointment upon the head, that ran down upon the beard, even Aaron's beard: that went down to the skirts of his garments; As the dew of Hermon, and as the dew that descended upon the mountains of Zion: for there the Lord commanded the blessing even life forevermore"*

When you love God's people, including the less privileged, automatically God's blessing will be attracted and released to you. If you desire to experience an unhindered flow of blessings, you must love unconditionally and live in harmony with others.

Take a look at Psalms 34 closely from verses 12-16. Verse 14 warned us to depart from evil and pursue peace, while verse 16 says the face of the Lord is against those who do evil.

Assurance Of God's Presence
Unity commands the presence of God. The spirit of God is a gentle spirit and doesn't dwell in an environment full of strife.

2 Corinthians 13:11 says, *"Finally, brethren, farewell. Be perfect, be of good comfort, be of one mind, live in peace; and the God of love and peace shall be with you."*

The Trinity will be with you whenever you make a commitment to walk in love and unity. The Holy Spirit who represents the presence of God is a gentle and peaceful spirit. Love attracts the presence of God to whoever makes a commitment to practice it. God is always flowing in an environment of love and unity. Whenever your love life is disrupted, you grieve the Holy Spirit and God doesn't dwell in a hostile environment.

1 John 4:12 says, *"No man hath seen God at any time. If we love one another, God dwelleth in us, and his love is perfected us."*

Good Health And Long Life

When you walk in the love of God and in unity, you will live a life void of sickness and disease. You will live in peace and joy. You will not be a partaker of some of the sicknesses caused by anger, bitterness, unforgiveness, and strife; because scientists have found that strife increases the risk of heart disease and stroke.

Love acts as a security for your life because the devil cannot penetrate a life full of love, peace, and joy.

Psalms 34:12-14 says, "What man is he that desireth life and loveth many days that he may see good? Keep thy tongue from evil and thy lips from speaking guile, depart from evil, and do good, seek peace and pursue it." The more you pursue peace with all men, the healthier you become.

Fear Is Destroyed

Being tormented by the devil is proof that your love for God and his people is questionable. You can't love and be fearful because love is bold. When you walk in love and unity, fear, which is the tool of the devil will be destroyed and cast out from your life.

Please understand this, I am not saying that only the fearful are being tormented by the devil. But you can resist the devil and cast the spirit of fear out of your life when you walk in love.

1 John 4:18; *"There is no fear in love; but perfect love casteth out fear: because fear hath torment. He that feareth is not made perfect in love."*

Strength To Cast Out The Devil

Being united and walking in love will make you more effective and efficient in dealing with the devil and taking dominion.

There is strength in love and unity. When you walk in agreement, you can bind the devil and cast him out easily. You can ask God for anything in agreement. He always honours His word.

Matthew 18:19-20 says, ***"Again I say unto you, that if two of you shall agree on earth as touching any thing that they shall ask, it shall be done for them of my Father which is in heaven. For where two or three are gathered together in my name, there am I in the midst of them."***

Deuteronomy 32:30: ***"How should one chase a thousand, and two put ten thousand to flight, except their Rock had sold them, and the Lord had shut them up."***

When you operate in love and unity, you position yourself for the power of the word in your life to destroy the devil and his cohorts.

Ecclesiastes 4:9-12: ***"Two are better than one; because they have a good reward for their labour For if they fall, the one will lift up his fellow: but woe to him that is alone when he falleth; for he hath not another to help him up. Again, if two lie together, then they have heat: but how can one be warm alone? And if one prevail against him, two shall withstand him; and a threefold cord is not quickly broken."***

Fullness of Joy and Pleasure

When you show love to one another by living a life above strife and bitterness, you will experience joy and pleasure all the time.

Psalm 16:11 says, *"Thou wilt show me the path of life: in thy presence is fullness of joy, at thy right hand there is pleasure for evermore."*

Evidence of Christianity

You will be respected in the society and people will see Jesus and His glory in your life. By coming together in love and unity, we showcase the love of Christ to the world.

John 13:35, *"By this shall all men know that ye are my disciples, if ye have love one to another.".*

Matthew 5:9; *"Blessed are the peacemakers for they will be called children of God.".*

CHAPTER FOUR

DANGERS AND EFFECTS OF STRIFE AND UNFORGIVENESS

Consequences of strife to individuals, the family, church, nation are enormous. It is a deadly enemy of destiny. It is a serious issue that needs to be addressed, warring against the spirit behind it.

Never live a lifestyle of strife and bitterness because it is an avenue that opens doors for Satan to tear relationships apart, kill, steal, and destroy (John 10:10). Your health will be affected negatively, unresolved conflict and disagreement will weaken your immune system, thereby exposing you to all kinds of health problems.

James 3:16, *"For where envying and strife is, there is confusion and every evil work."*

God wants us to avoid strife like a plague because it is deadly and spreads like a cancer. Love is the antidote to strife and is not negotiable if you want to see strife flee from your life. Go through the benefits of walking in love in chapter three to discover the amazing and mysterious things love can do for you.

Some months ago, my husband on his way to the office decided to stop at the bank to check why he couldn't get credits for drafts submitted for repurchase more than seven months prior. It led to an argument when he insisted that he must get the credit before leaving the bank.

Less than five minutes after leaving the bank, he ran into road and traffic control officers who took him to their office and wasted his whole day over an offense that would have usually earned a simple warning.

The dictionary defines strife as 'conflict, disappointment, friction, or bad feelings.' It is easy to understand, from the definition, why the Bible condemns strife. It reduces potency of prayers. Love and strife are mutually exclusive; it is either you are in love or in strife. Where there is no love, there is no home. It is just a habitation. It ruins homes, churches, communities, and nations.

Apart from constituting a danger to your health, let's look at other dangers strife produces.

1. *Strife reduces the power of prayers.* Jesus stressed the importance and the efficacy of the prayers of agreement in Matthew 18:19. This is why the devil works so hard to create division and disharmony among believers in churches, families, communities, etc, so that he can reduce the efficacy of their prayers.

If we find ourselves in conflict with someone, we should reconcile and seek GOD for forgiveness. Apart from that, when you are in strife, you will find it very difficult to pray because of the burden and bitterness in your heart. A bitter heart hinders communication flow with God.

2. *Lack of growth and development.* God cannot dwell in a polluted environment. Churches or families where strife exist cannot grow or develop spiritually. It is love that bind siblings, couples, churches, and nations together, but strife tears them apart.

3. *It is a faith destroyer.* Faith works by love. When strife comes in, love disappears. Love is an essential supplement to faith. When you are a contentious couple with unforgiveness, your faith will be oscillating rather than moving mountains.

4.   *Strife takes away lives and properties.* There are communities that will never recover from the effect of strife and violence. The impact of civil strife in some communities that destroy lives and properties cannot be over-emphasized. I have seen some partners kill their spouses because of strife. Some individuals are in the hospital and some on wheelchairs as a result of strife and unforgiveness.

In a nutshell, all believers must avoid conflict, discord, or disagreement in your relationships in order to see the glory of God. Shun strife and embrace forgiveness at all times.

OVERCOMING STRIFE AND OFFENCES
Do not meddle with strife; it is spiritual in nature and comes from the devil. It is a tool to control, manipulate, kill, steal, and destroy marriages, businesses, churches, communities, and nations; even your own self.

If you want to walk in the power of God twenty-four seven, you must make an effort to overcome strife and offenses.

The following points will help you stand against strife whenever it shows up.

Develop A Shock Absorber To Strife

Let it sink into your memory that offenses will come; you can't avoid it as long as you live in the midst of people.

Even though Jesus placed a curse upon the offender, you are bound to be offended or offend people. Don't let it take you by surprise when it happens. Learn how to overlook and forgive in advance. Like one of my fathers in the Lord said, you should look at the situation as Jesus would have looked at it.

It is not all issues we should regard as offences, there are things we trash without procrastinating. Do you know you can actually disagree with someone without it leading to strife? At times we need to agree to disagree and still love one another.

Develop Your Spirit

Strife is a product of carnality. It comes as a result of an unregenerated spirit and is the work of the flesh. You may not be able to overcome strife or offenses unless your spirit is developed against it. The flesh needs to be subdued continually.

Galatians 5:19-21 describes strife as the work of the flesh. To overcome the flesh, there is need to constantly renew our mind like Paul admonished us in Romans 12:1-2; *"I beseech you therefore, brethren, by the mercies of God, that you present your bodies as a living sacrifice, holy, acceptable to God, which is your reasonable service. And do not be conformed to this world, but be transformed by the renewing of your mind, that you may prove what is that good and acceptable and perfect will of God."*

How do you renew your mind? By constantly feeding and meditating on the word of God, listening to good messages of anointed men of God, and reading Christian novels. While the flesh cannot accommodate insults or foolish talk and wants to fulfil its lustful desires by retaliating at all cost, you must not make provision for it.

Romans 13:13-14, *"Let us walk properly, as in the day, not in revelry and drunkenness, not in lewdness and lust, not in strife and envy. But put on the Lord Jesus Christ, and make no provision for the flesh, to fulfil its lusts."*

Be Sensitive To The Holy Spirit
Pray for the power of discernment to detect strife. The ability to identify strife coming will pave a way for you to isolate, resist, and stand against it.

Guard Your Heart

Proverbs 4:23, *"Keep thy heart with all diligence, for out of it are the issues of life."*

Your heart determines the course of your life. Your thought life and your emotions will control the rest of your life, because a man's attitude leads to his actions.

Proverbs 23:7, *"As a man thinketh in his heart so he is."*

If you want to avoid strife, you must be determined to guard your mind. A man that commits murder did not develop murderous thoughts on the day of the crime. The thought must have been previously harboured in his heart for a certain period.

Matthew 15:19 says, *"For out of the heart proceed evil thoughts, murder, adulteries, fornication, thefts, false witness, blasphemies."*

The more I study the word of God, the more I hate strife and the more I want to love people. Control your thoughts by thinking only positive thoughts and the word of God. Store up the word of God in your heart. It has the power to cleanse, transform, and keep you from strife. It is powerful enough to keep you from the horrors of strife.

Cast down every imagination of bitterness, anger, murder, and strife whenever they show up in your thought life.

James 3:14, *"Who is a wise man and endued with knowledge among you? let him shew out of a good conversation his works with meekness of wisdom."*

Never leave the door of your heart open to junk. Your heart is a battlefield; don't allow the devil to sow seeds of discord into your heart. What you think is what you become; think about divorce and you will soon be divorced, think about strife and you will soon encounter somebody to fight with.

Amazingly, the word of the Lord is powerful enough for you to think positively if you store it in your heart.

Hebrews 4:12, *"For the word of God is quick, and powerful, and sharper than any two-edged sword, piercing even to the dividing asunder of soul and spirit, and of the joints and marrow, and is a discerner of the thoughts and intents of the heart."*

Speak Against It

Strife and offence destroy marriages and other human relationships. They must be handled spiritually and are mountains that must be spoken to and cast into the sea. You too can take authority over the spirit of strife and offence.

Jesus instructed us to speak to our mountain in Mark 11:23, ***"For verily I say unto you, that whosoever shall say unto this mountain, be thou removed and be thou cast into the sea; and shall not doubt in his heart, but shall believe that those things which he saith shall come to pass; he shall have whatsoever he saith."***

When you sense strife and offence sneaking into your marriage or into your life, begin to take authority over such by praying as follows:

Spirit of strife, you are not permitted to operate in my marriage or in my life. I cast you out of my family in the name of Jesus. I declare that I am loving, I am patient, I am a child of God that is ruled by the fruit of the Spirit and not by the flesh. I call forth unity and love into my marriage. I declare I am not a product of the flesh but of the Spirit. The flesh is not permitted to rule me in the name of Jesus.

Use your Word-given authority to deal with strife whenever it shows up, period! It will find its level. Treat strife and bitterness as spirits that need to be bound and cast to the sea. Myself and my husband have spoken to strife to get out from our family when we are in disagreement on certain issues.

Embrace Humility And Shun Pride

Luke 14:11, *"For whoever exalts himself will be humbled and he who humbles himself will be exalted."*

Meekness goes beyond unity. Meekness is the ability to endure injury with patience and without retaliation. Humility is the basic requirement to live a victorious life. It will make you cater to the betterment of others and not place your priority above theirs.

Humility moves you to fight for others. When you hurt someone, you humble yourself before the person and realize your faults. Pride breaks our intimacy with God. It is the source of war, anger, strife, insult, abusive words, and contentions.

Proverbs 13:10 [NIV], *"Where there is strife, there*

is pride, but wisdom is found in those who take advice."

Pride will keep you from saying sorry when you are wrong. Learn to admit your faults whenever you err.

Embrace The Fruit Of The Spirit

The works of the flesh, if allowed to germinate in your life, will be hurtful to yourself and others around you; so, let's endeavour to embrace the renewed nature, bearing the fruit of the Spirit, to take possession of our lives. This will make us shun and run away from strife.

Galatians 5:22-23, *"But the fruit of the Spirit is love, joy, peace, long-suffering gentleness, goodness, faith, meekness, temperance; against such there is no law."*

CHAPTER FIVE

TOTAL FORGIVENESS

God will not tell you to do what you don't have the ability to do. Total forgiveness is to forgive those who wrong you as if nothing happened like Jesus did. He forgave and cleaned up your record of offences.

Your ability to forgive is only achievable if you make the right decision by the help of the Holy Spirit.

1 Peter 3:9 (Amplified Version); *"Never return evil for evil or insult for insult (scolding, tongue- lashing, berating), but on the contrary blessing [praying for their welfare, happiness, and protection, and truly pitying and loving them]. For know that to this you have been called, that you may yourselves inherit a blessing [from God–that you may obtain a blessing as heirs, bringing welfare and happiness and protection]."*

As obedient believers, who want to make Heaven and constantly receiving from God, we cannot afford to hold anything against anyone. Make up your mind to pursue peace at all times. We must be determined not to indulge in unforgiveness in our hearts. If you refuse to forgive, you will not be able to receive any breakthrough or spectacular miracle from your Maker. Forgiveness is the key to our inheritance, deliverance, healing, and prosperity. It is also an antidote to sin and central to all aspects of life.

It is time to stop walking around, discussing how you were mistreated or wounded by relatives, close friends, associates, or betrayed by pastors you loved or your spouse. You don't need to get mad at them anymore; instead, pray for them by committing them to God to change them. Ask God to bless them and their families. Pray that the Holy Spirit will help you to be free from resentment and give you grace to forgive. You can pray Ephesians 1:16-21 prayer for them.

"Cease not to give thanks for you, making mention of you in my prayers; That the God of our Lord Jesus Christ, the Father of glory, may give unto you the spirit of wisdom and revelation in the knowledge of him: The eyes of your understanding being enlightened; that ye may know what is the hope of

his calling, and what the riches of the glory of his inheritance in the saints, and what is the exceeding greatness of his power to usward who believe, according to the working of his mighty power, which he wrought in Christ when he raised him from the dead, and set him at his own right hand in heavenly places."

Make a commitment to pray blessings into the life of the person who has offended you. Pray to God to give them the spirit of wisdom and revelation in the knowledge of Him. Tell God to open the eyes of their understanding. Ask God also to have mercy on them just as He has had mercy on you. Pray that you do not remember and take account of the offenses they committed against you, just like Jesus doesn't remember your sins anymore.

Hebrews 8:12, *"For I will be merciful to their unrighteousness, and their sins and their iniquities will I remember no more."*

"Funke, it's like you don't understand what I went through in the hands of these relatives of mine and my close friends. They offended me and stole my inheritance."

Relax. I understand what you are going through. But as long as you refuse to forgive and walk in

love, you will be allowing the devil to steal further from you. Let's take a look at Matthew 5:23-24;
"Therefore, if thou bring thy gift to the altar and there remember that thy brother ought against thee, leave there thy gift before the altar and go thy way, first be reconciled to thy brother and then come and offer thy gift?"

God Himself frowns at your offering when you are not walking in forgiveness. If anybody sins or offends you, forgive easily. Don't allow any thought of bitterness spring up in your heart. Unforgiveness and bitterness will defile you and trouble your spirit. Do you know that you do yourself greater harm when you keep malice and refuse to let go of offenses from your heart?

Biblical forgiveness is to forget completely and never keep record of wrongs like God does against you. God justified you, pardoned you, forgave you, sanctified you, and declared you righteous in His sight and before men. Let me assure you that the devil will continue to cause havoc in your body as long as you walk in bitterness, unforgiveness, and resentment towards those who offend you.

I was in that situation before. I had been defrauded and mistreated by very close friends, who used their exalted positions to mistreat me. They pushed me into bitterness, anger, and severe resentment. I was bitter about their negative attitude towards me. In the process, my body began to malfunction. I had physical and emotional pain and started running from one hospital to another. My health was in jeopardy.

Before that time, I had never had any health challenge. I thought I was going to die. I realized where I missed it and made a U-turn. I chose to forgive and let go.

It is time for all believers to learn the power of forgiveness and begin to put it to work in your life. You must not allow your prayer to be hindered or your health to be in shambles because you harbour bitterness, malice, and unforgiveness in your heart.

The easiest way for the devil to steal your joy, miracle, and health is through unforgiveness and bitterness. If you want your prayers to be answered, consider this Bible passage:

Mark 11:25, *"And when ye stand praying, forgive, if ye ought against any that your father also which is in heaven may forgive you your trespasses."*

BIBLICAL EXAMPLES OF TOTAL FORGIVENESS AND RECONCILIATION: JACOB AND ESAU

Jacob, twin brother to Esau, decided to steal the family blessing meant for Esau with the help of his mother, Rebecca. The deceitful and cunning action offended Esau and he vowed to kill Jacob.

Genesis. 27:41b, *"And Esau hated Jacob because of the blessing where with his father blessing him; and Esau said in heart, the days of mourning for my father are at hand, then will I slay my brother Jacob."*

Jacob fled to the land of Haran because his life was in jeopardy. After 20 years with Laban in a foreign land, he was commanded by God to return home. Jacob knew that having an encounter with Esau would be tense and not easy. Wracked with fear, he sent messengers with enormous gifts to his brother to pacify and appease him before his arrival.

Jacob had wrestled with God at Bethel and repented of his sin, and received salvation. God promised him protection in his father's country of Canaan.

At last ,the moment of encounter arrived. Esau surprised him with an embrace and he fell on his face and kissed his brother. In doing that, the impending tension and anxiety by Esau was broken. The open wound was healed. Both of them wept together, Esau graciously tried to reject the gift from Jacob, but he insisted he accept them.

The transformed Jacob who met God and received his blessing amid the struggle equally received a new name, Israel, and renamed the location where he had seen God as a sign of honour to the Almighty Father.

Genesis 32:30, *"And Jacob called the name of the place Peniel: for I have seen God face to face, and my life is preserved."*

When our relationship with people is severed, our relationship with God will also have cracks. Both relationships are inseparable.

Esau's attitude in greeting his brother in an affectionate manner is remarkable and shows the epitome of humility and forgiveness which we must emulate.

JOSEPH AND HIS FAMILY
Joseph forgave his brothers for selling him to

slavery at the age of seventeen. It was hurtful and painful for Joseph to be separated from his siblings in such a manner. There had been a strained and broken relationship between Joseph and his brothers for years because of envy, especially after God had showed him a blueprint of his future.

Fulfilling His word, while in Egypt, God took him from slavery and imprisonment to a position of authority, where He was used mightily to deliver his family from famine. Upon seeing his brothers, he didn't retaliate against them, though he had the opportunity to. He chose to forgive them, having seen the power of God who turned the counsel of enemies in his favour.

God is in the business of turning any circumstance to work for our good as expressed in Romans 8:28, ***"And we know that all things work together for good to them that love God, to them who are the called according to his purpose."***

Joseph showed the example of our Lord Jesus Christ, who chose to forgive us rather than punish us for the many sins we have committed. He decided to bear sin on our behalf; as a result, God does not see sin and failure in us, but the righteousness of God in Christ Jesus. Joseph never saw their sins anymore but gave God the glory.

Genesis 45:4-5, *"And Joseph said unto his brethren, Come near to me, I pray you. And they came near. And he said, I am Joseph your brother, whom ye sold into Egypt. Now therefore be not grieved, nor angry with yourselves, that ye sold me hither: for God did send me before you to preserve life."*

NO LEGAL LIMIT ON FORGIVENESS

Peter wanted to know how many times he had to wait before he could retaliate when offended, thinking seven times would be appropriate. But Jesus makes us understand there is no legal limit to forgiveness. It is unlimited.

Matthew 18:21-22, *"Then came Peter to him, and said, Lord, how oft shall my brother sin against me and I forgive him? Till seven times? Jesus said unto him, I say not unto thee, until seven times: but until seventy times seven."*

Wow! Incredible! 490 times for man to forgive! Is it per day? Per week? Per month? Per year? Honestly, I don't know. If it is per year, we have only 365 or 366 days in a year. No man is capable of offending his fellow man 490 times in this period.

Christians are to forgive continually without limit over and over again. We don't have a choice when it comes to forgiveness. It is not negotiable no matter the grievance or offence.

Colossians 3:13 states, *"For bearing one another and forgiving one another if any man have a quarrel against any; even as Christ forgave you, so also do ye."*

All believers must pattern their lives after Jesus, who gave the same forgiveness to us. Jesus is the greatest forgiver and easily forgave those who crucified Him. He asked the Father to forgive them, because they don't know what they do. What can be more grievous than the offence committed against Jesus? You must extend grace and undeserved favour to the offender like that which God extends to you.

If you yourself want freedom from the bondage of your own unforgiving attitude, then don't allow yourself to be trapped in resentment, anger, pain, and suffering that strife and unforgiveness can cause. Forgiveness is a choice a believer must make to release their offender from the shackles of pain. You cannot walk in love and walk in strife. They are two parallel lines that cannot meet and mutually exclusive.

It is better to walk in forgiveness and love than walking in hatred or bitterness. You may ask this question: "What if they refuse to forgive me, despite the fact that I have forgiven them?"

Go through the principle of reconciliation in Chapter Seven. If it doesn't work, that is their cup of tea. You are simply to obey God, forgive, forget, and move on with your life. Don't blindly allow the devil to rip you of your blessings by using a negative attitude towards people.

FORGIVENESS, RESTORATION, AND ASSOCIATION OF A RELATIONSHIP

Every believer must explore every possibility to restore broken relationships. While the Bible encourages forgiveness and restoration of strained relationships, not all strained relationships can lead to association after a period of strife.

It is possible to reconcile without association. While love is a command, association is by choice. Love preaches restoration, but not all reconciliations can bring back association as not all associations are healthy for our Christian pilgrimage.

Some associations after reconciliation and

forgiveness can expose you to more danger and wounds. There are also associations that the Bible warned us about, to come out and be separated from.

2 Corinthians 6:14-17, *"Be ye not unequally yoked together with unbelievers for what fellowship hath righteousness with unrighteousness? And what communion hath light with darkness.? And what concord hath Christ with belial? Or what part hath he that believeth with an infidel? And what agreement hath the temple of God with Idols? For ye are the temple of the living God, as God hath said, I will dwell in them, and walk in them, and will be their God, and they shall be my people. Wherefore come out from among them, and be ye separate said the Lord, and touch not the unclean thing, and I will receive thee."*

Apostle Paul warned the Corinthian Christians to avoid fellow believers who live immoral lives in 1 Corinthians 5:9-13. We should also be careful about the company we keep.

Proverbs 12:26 NKJV, *"The righteous should choose his friends carefully, for the way of the wicked leads them astray."*

Love and forgiveness are quite different from association. For example, to restore a relationship after someone has been cheated on, betrayed, or abused is not easy. Some relationships will never return to normal after been damaged by strife.

Come to think of it, what kind of association can an abused teenager and her abuser have? Should your teenager continue living with such people? What kind of association can you have with a business partner that defrauded or betrayed you? Do you want to continue doing business with such a person if he has not repented?

Practically speaking, such associations may be ruptured forever, especially if the offender has not repented. You cannot continue keeping company with unrepentant sinners. You are not permitted to be yoked together with them, but come out and be separated.

In such contexts, only forgiveness is achievable, not association. You can leave the relationship and still love them. It is not mandatory to continue with a relationship where you are not compatible, spiritually or otherwise. Since God commands us to forgive, you must do so without remembering the offenses anymore.

When sin is blotted out, it is same as covering a writing or picture with ink or paint. They cannot be seen anymore. That is the way our Lord Jesus Christ erased our transgression.

Isaiah 44:22, *"I have blotted out, like a thick cloud, your transgressions, And like a cloud, your sins. Return to Me, for I have redeemed you."*

Isaiah 43:25, *"I, even I, am He who blots out your transgressions for My own sake; and I will not remember your sins."*

His word promises that He forgives and forgets our offenses. In the same vein, you should pray to God for the help to forgive and extend such grace to your offenders.

CHAPTER SIX

FORGETTING THE PAST

In a man's lifetime, he is bound to be hurt, betrayed, or offended one way or the other. But what he does with the offences reveal his maturity and determines his destiny in life.

If your heart is filled with pain, hurt, and resentment, it will be difficult to move on with a new life or new opportunity. Whenever you hold on to the past, Satan will hold on to your future and perpetually hang around you to cause more havoc. Our past is passed forever. Therefore, a man must learn not to torment himself for past sins or hurts.

There are people today who dwell on things in the past, which cannot be changed or altered, thereby causing them to constantly remember these bad memories or old wounds and perpetually stay stuck, not moving forward. The more you replay the memories of the past the angrier you become.

Your past can be a tool to better the opportunities in your life, if you are determined not to allow it to affect you or determine your future. But I assure you, you can make use of these to your own advantage.

Just as you read earlier, I have been wounded, deeply hurt, and betrayed by close friends. At the end, it worked to my advantage; it birthed this very book, opened my eyes to many opportunities in life, and made me wiser and smarter in future dealings and endeavours.

You cannot recreate the pain or loss of yesterday. You can only refuse to process it and do something to change your tomorrow by repositioning yourself; it doesn't matter how long. Our Father in heaven is a God of new things and willing to open new chapters in your life.

Isaiah 43:19 says, *"Behold I will do a new thing, now it shall spring forth; shall ye not know it? I will even make a way in the wilderness and rivers in the desert."*

He is loving enough to forget and forgive your past errors or mistakes, if you yourself are ready to let go.

How do you forget past offenses and hurt in

preparation to moving forward with a new life? I think l can help you with practical steps which the Holy Spirit showed me. It really helped in the healing process.

1. Be Determined To Forgive Those Who Offend You

Remember, forgiveness is not a gift, but a choice you need to make in life if you really want to walk with God. Although difficult, we need to walk in the grace of God to get better and not bitter. Be determined and willing to forgive, like Jesus, those who have offended you despite the gravity of the offense.

The real believer must be obedient to the word of God and must deny himself for the sake of seeking and pursuing peace. This is the only way to freedom and a healthy life.

2. Renew Your Mind With The Word Of God

During my ordeal, I spent much time in the word of God and began to experience emotional healing. Instead of replaying memories of the past, get acquainted with the word of God concerning the love of God into your heart.

Romans 12:2, *"And be not conformed to this world: but be ye transformed by the renewing of your mind, that ye may prove what is that good, and acceptable, and perfect, will of God."*

The more positive words you have in your heart, the easier it will be to control your thoughts and negative emotions. Inject the word of God regularly into your spirit; it has the ability to purify your thoughts.

The word of God has the ability to heal, just as described in Proverbs 4:20-22 (AMP), *"My son, attend to my words; consent and submit to my sayings. Let them not depart from your sight; keep them in the center of your heart, For they are life to those who find them, healing and health to all their flesh."*

3. Take It To God In Prayer

You need to pray for your own sins as well. You need to ask God to forgive you for harbouring offenses for so long and allowing it to fester in your heart.

After doing that, table the offense(s) before God and ask Him to take over your heart. Forgive those who have offended you and don't dwell on it again, just like our Lord Jesus Christ who never remembers our iniquities.

Hebrews 8:12: *"For I will be merciful to their unrighteousness and their sins and their lawless deeds I will remember no more".*

Ask the Holy Spirit to purify you from any offence and help you forget the past when you recall the hurt. Ask the Holy Spirit to give you the ability to let go of grudges and offenses. He is kind and always available to ease your burden and pain. Ask Him to use your hurt and pain for His glory.

4. *Pray For The Offender*
How does God want us to respond to people who hurt us?

We follow Jesus' example in forgiveness; we pray for those who offend or insult us. Practically speaking, you may find it very difficult to pray for those who offend you. It would take a lot of strength and maturity not to retaliate, but choose to play the fool and break the cycle in a different way.

The way things operate in the kingdom of God is different from what is obtainable in the world. In the wisdom of the world, nobody who offends or insults you should go free without retaliation.

However, in God's kingdom, you do not retaliate but pay back with a blessing.

1 Peter 3:9, *"Not rendering evil for evil, or railing: but contrariwise blessing; knowing that ye are thereunto called, that ye should inherit a blessing."*

Luke 6:27-29, *"But I say to you who hear: Love your enemies, do good to those who hate you, bless those who curse you, and pray for those who spitefully use you. To him who strikes you on the one cheek, offer the other also. And from him who takes away your cloak, do not withhold your tunic either."*

How do you love or pray for somebody that abused you or your child? How do you love a foster mother that maltreated you badly? How do you pray or love a friend that betrayed and defrauded you? How do you love and pray for armed robbers that raided your house and raped your child?

What if they are co-pastors or church leaders who betrayed, defrauded, or hurt you deeply instead of showing you love? How do you love and pray for the husband that nearly beat you to death? How do you love and pray for those who curse you and continue in their hurtful behaviour?

God wants you to pray for and love them! Period! When God asks you to do something that you find difficult, knowing your weakness on that particular issue, there is a need to ask for strength from above to do what He asks. Ask God to supply the power and strength to pray and love them.

One night, in pain, hurt, and resentful at what my close friends had done to me, I was weeping again. I cried to the Holy Spirit to soften my heart and give me the strength and power to pray for these people and supply the energy to be kind and patient with them.

That particular night, I was filled with the Holy Ghost and God began to give me prayer points which I jotted down to use in praying for them, along with a verse, Ephesians 6:7, *"With good will, doing service as to the Lord, and not to men."*

That particular year, I travelled to the United States and returned with good packaged shirts as a token of kindness for two of these people who I was close to before the misunderstanding happened. I began to show them love and kindness by not going down the path of revenge in my thoughts. I began to speak to them over the phone once in a while until the relationship was restored.

On a daily basis, I began to pray for them. The more I prayed, the more I loved them, and the more my body restored. When you choose to pray and bless those who hurt you, these are powerful tools of protection which you will need to keep you from becoming bitter, hateful, and bent on revenge.

5. Embrace The Holy Spirit For Direction

After you have been betrayed, hurt, or offended, ask the Holy Spirit to show you the right course of action. Let Him be your guide. Proverbs 3:5, *"Trust in the Lord with all thine heart and lean not unto thine own understanding; in all thy ways acknowledge him, and he shall direct thy path."*

Never take a step without His direction so that you will not make further mistakes or errors. Be a friend to the Holy Spirit, as He is able to supply the strength and ability to forgive. He will tell you the kind of prayer you need to pray concerning those who hurt you. He may ask you to write a book filled with your experiences in order to help others. He may tell you to set up a foundation for abused teenagers. He may equally tell you how to reconcile with the offender. Ask God to expand your horizon.

6. Praise Him Regularly

Your regular praise unto God can make you forget the past. Praise is an antidote for the spirit of heaviness. When you are depressed and molested, cloth yourself with the garment of praise.

Isaiah 61:3, *"To appoint unto them that mourn in Zion, to give unto them beauty for ashes, the oil of joy for mourning, the garment of praise for the spirit of heaviness; that they might be called trees of righteousness, the planting of the LORD, that he might be glorified."*

7. Never Keep Track Record of Offenses

Or to put it another way, "Forgive and forget." This may look impossible because our brain has the capacity to store and keep memories. As humans, painful memories cannot be deleted. But the Bible says, love keeps no record of wrong.

"Love is not ill-mannered or selfish or irritable; love does not keep a record of wrongs."
1 Corinthians 13:5 (GNB)

Forgive every day and follow God's example by having a forgiving heart that overlooks offenses.

101

When you do this, you are not permitted to reopen or keep discussing these issues with a third party.

God wants all His children to possess a forgiving spirit and forgive your offender if you want to enjoy an unhindered flow of blessings and fellowship with God. Stop speaking to those who hurt you about how you've being hurt. Rather, choose to speak a kind word, choose to be patient, and choose to do good to them.

Ephesians 4:32 says, *"Be kind and compassionate to one another, forgiving each other just as Christ in God forgave you."*

HOW TO TURN YOUR PAST HURT INTO A FORTUNE

An unwillingness to forget the past will keep you from going forward. As stated earlier, you cannot change yesterday; but you can do something to change your tomorrow. Don't allow a hurtful past to affect your future negatively but positively. You will get trapped in one position if you refuse to lay aside all hurts, pain, offenses, and problems that can easily set you back in the journey of life.

God permits certain circumstances to come our way. He wants us to learn from and not to be imprisoned by them.

Apostle Paul reaffirms this in Philippians 3:13, *"Brethren, I count not myself to have apprehended; but this one thing I do, forgetting those things which are behind and reaching forth unto things which are before, I press toward the mark for the prize of the high calling of God in Christ Jesus."*

In every negative circumstance, there is always something positive to learn. Beyond what should be learnt, each contains what is needed to turn the situation into pleasure or gain. To achieve this, however, you need to reject all labels of past misfortune and not hold on to hatred and resentment, which only poison you.

Romance 8:28, *"And we know that all things work together for good to them that love God, to them who are called according to His purpose."*

Jeremiah 29:11 says, *"I know the plans I have for you declare the Lord plan of peace, not of evil, to give you an expected end."*

God does not have any negative purpose for our hurts and suffering. He can only use it for His glory. Our pain can be used to refine or draw us closer to Him, which will in-turn launch us to our desired goal.

You need to arise above every circumstance and walk into the greatest life God has given to you; He has a purpose for your life.

Let's examine below how we can turn past hurt into fortune.

Stop Reacting To Offenses

Respond to hurts or offenses rather than reacting to them. Stop blaming anybody for the abuse or betrayal you experienced, or whatever might have come your way. Face the challenge and keep moving forward.

Believe In Yourself

You can turn your pain into a fortune by believing in what God can use you to do. Many people have relegated their lives thinking they can't become who God created them to be. You have to remove the word 'can't' from your vocabulary. Stop doubting yourself by believing that you cannot be good enough to become better in life.

Cultivate a biblical mentality, discover who you are in the Bible. Declare what God has written concerning you.

- You have been redeemed from being natural to being supernatural.

• You have been redeemed from the shackles of failure to success.

• You have been adopted unto a family of success where failure is not an option.

• You can do all things through Christ who strengthens you!

Don't hang around those who are negative.
There are lots of people who never believe in possibilities. They will quench your idea and discourage you from taking a step or risk. They will make you feel life is not worth living.

Just because they failed in marriage doesn't mean marriage is not good. Just because they failed in business doesn't mean everybody is failing. They say, "The country is bad; you can't make it here" when other people are succeeding in the same country.

Don't allow such people to poison your mind and bring you to a state of hopelessness. Surround yourself with people who are optimistic and positive. Spend time with goal-getters and those who can inspire you to be better. They will bring out the best in you and bring you up when you are down.

CHAPTER SEVEN

PRINCIPLES OF BIBLICAL CONFLICT RESOLUTION

Conflict is inevitable in the society, family, and even among believers. Even God knows there will be misunderstandings. He hates offenses although He knows they will surely come.

Conflict can be between husband and wife, among siblings, even among brethren in the church, and so on. As you are all aware, the purpose of strife or conflict is to rupture relationships. Where there is no unity, there can be no progress, peace, or love.

Amos 3:3, *"Can two walk together except they be agreed?"*

The easiest way for the devil to weaken your power and progress is through strife and bitterness. Resolving conflicts can be difficult, but God wants us to pursue peace at all costs and stay away from strife or evil actions.

Hebrews 12:14, *"Follow peace with all men and holiness, without which no man shall see the Lord."* God has pronounced a blessing upon the peacemaker.

Matthew 5:9, *"Blessed are the peace makers, for they shall be called the sons of God."*

God desires that we avoid all strife instead of engaging in them. You must endeavour to maintain a forgiving attitude towards one another by exploring every avenue available to resolving conflict.

1 Peter 3:9 (AMP), *"Never return evil for evil or insult for insult (scolding, tongues lashing, berating), but on the contrary blessing (praying for their welfare, happiness and protection, and truly pitying and loving them). For know that to this you have been called, that you may yourselves inherit a blessing (from God - that you may obtain a blessing as heirs, bringing welfare and happiness and protection)."*

God frowns at your offering when you are in strife. He says there is need to reconcile with your brother before your offering can be acceptable.

Matthew 5:23-24, *"Therefore if thou bring thy gift to the altar, and there rememberest that thy brother hath ought against thee; Leave there thy gift before the altar, and go thy way; first be reconciled to thy brother, and then come and offer thy gift."*

A believer who wants to make Heaven and wants God to answer his/her prayers cannot afford conflicts without resolutions. Let's examine a few of these options and guidelines God has provided for resolving conflicts which every believer should follow.

PRINCIPLE NUMBER ONE:

Initiate the Idea in Private

This is the easiest and most common way to resolve conflict. This is by letting the offending brother or party know his/her fault privately, not discussing it with others. You are to say the matter kindly and show him his conduct. By doing that, both parties can reconcile privately within themselves, without calling a third party or referring the case to church leaders or family elders.

The principle of this rule should be practiced by all, under all circumstances, especially between husband and wife. They must learn how to resolve a problem in their bedroom before going to a third party. If you are able to follow this principle, the Bible says you have done more service to Him than even justice to yourself.

Matthew 18:15, *"Moreover, if thy brother shall trespass against thee, go and tell his fault between thee and him alone. If he shall hear thee, thou shall gain thy brother."*

PRINCIPLE NUMBER TWO:
With A Witness

If principle number one fails, the Bible says take two or three witness during reconciliation. By having two or three to talk to the offending party, the person's heart may become softened and guided towards reconciliation.

Matthew 18:16, *"If he will not hear thee, then take with thee one or two more that in the mouth of two or three witnesses, every word may be established."*

PRINCIPLE NUMBER THREE:

Before The Church

In a case where the principles above fail, you need to let the church authorities be aware of the matter.

Matthew 18:17, *"And if he shall neglect to hear them bring the case to the church authority to which both belong."*

You may ask me, what if the other party is not from my church? You need to trace his church and report the matter to his pastor. Many people outside our church have reported our church members to us; and to the glory of God, within the church councils, we were able to resolve their issues.

PRINCIPLE NUMBER FOUR:
Seek The Face Of God For Further Direction

This is the last principle the Bible says we should adopt in conflict resolution. Having tried all the principles above, it is best to pray and seek the face of God for further direction. Pray for the offending brother regularly asking for God's mercy. Although the Bible says you should no longer regard him as a Christian brother but as a heathen or publican who you must break all associations with. You can aggressively pray for the offending party. It is almost impossible to stay angry with someone you pray for regularly.

My family had a similar experience. We refused to allow strife or dispute ruin our business and our lives; so, we decided to set aside our own hurt, anger, and bitterness to pursue peace with our fellow believers. We used all the principles above to resolve a dispute between us and a friend [also a pastor].

Despite the involvement of our senior pastor who travelled down to the country to resolve the conflict, it was to no avail. I and my husband moved a step further by inviting one of the erring pastors in a bid to seek reconciliation. He had felt offended by our not agreeing with his terms. We pleaded for forgiveness, despite the fact that we had not offended him.

In conclusion, we asked him to pray for our family and our business. In spite of my husband being far older than the erring pastor, in humility and a spirit of reconciliation, we knelt down in front of the pastor to pray for and forgive us.

After the prayer, we embraced one another and returned his plot of land which he had lost to the estate. We hoped that by taking this step, it would close the matter. This was done to pacify him and in the spirit of forgiveness and restoration.

He never showed up to claim the land, nor did he collect his deposit commitment or have anything to do with us despite our several calls. After two years of waiting, we sought counsel regarding the next line of action. In a nutshell, we were counselled and we decided to make a draft of his deposit and post it to him via a courier service; God commands us not to owe any man.

God has no pleasure in strife or dispute. You can't force anybody to love or forgive you. Just do what is possible to make peace and forgive those who offend you.

Do what the Bible says and lay the rest at the feet of Jesus and move on with your life. In the words of Proverbs 22:24, *"Make no friendship with an angry man and with a furious man thou shalt not go."*

HOW TO HANDLE STRIFE IN THE CHURCH

Many believe that the church is an environment that should be free from strife and discord, but I want you to realize that conflict is inevitable. As a matter of fact, strife or conflict is a reality in every church, regardless of whether it is a young, old, small, or large church.

Strife is the work of the flesh and an evidence of carnality in the soul of an unregenerated spirit.

The Corinthians were reproved for their contention in 1 Corinthians 3:1-3, *"And I, brethren, could not speak unto you as unto spiritual, but as unto carnal, even as unto babes in Christ. I have fed you with milk, and not with meat: for hitherto ye were not able to bear it, neither yet now are ye able. For ye are yet carnal: for whereas there is among you envying and strife and divisions, are ye not carnal and walk as men?"*

Satan's major tool used to put the church in disarray is strife, knowing fully it can hinder the move of God and the growth of the church. His job is to kill, steal, and destroy. This he accomplishes through sowing the seed of discord, gossip, rumours in the church. This is why we must be vigilant and jealously guard unity and peace in the church.

Church conflicts could be between fellow church members. It could also be in form of disagreements within its leadership, or issues of misconduct such as misappropriation of funds. It could also be regarding brethren who indulge in sinful behaviour such as those mentioned in 1 Corinthians 5:11: *"But now I have written unto you not to keep company, if any man that is called a brother be a fornicator, or covetous, or an idolater, or a railer, or a drunkard, or an extortioner."*

How do we respond to conflict in the congregation?

Our goal in resolving conflict is not to win arguments or arouse sympathy, but to confront sin, resolve conflict, reconcile with and win fellow believers to be restored back to God and the church. Conflict in the church can be handled easily when done prayerfully.

Practically speaking, not all conflict can be handled the same way. Each conflict has its own peculiarity, and pastors or leaders must be proactive in handling conflict in a way that honours God.

I watched a video on Facebook recently that involved a couple in a particular church planning to get married. Two weeks to the wedding, after printing their invitation cards, the pastor discovered that the relationship was based on deceit. They were already living together and the brother in question was already married; his wife resided in Europe and he had a child.

The pastor brought them out on a particular Sunday and narrated the whole story to the congregation. The couple were humiliated and disgraced publicly. The pastor, in annoyance, tore their membership certificates and banned them from the church premises.

There was no wisdom in handling the matter. Though the marriage ceremony was dissolved immediately, our Lord Jesus never handled a case like that. The situation could have been resolved in a better way which would have led to repentance, without their losing their souls to the devil.

Galatians 6:1 (NIV), *"Brothers and sisters, if someone is caught in a sin, you who live by the spirit should restore that person gently. But watch yourselves, or you also may be tempted."*

Expulsion from the congregation doesn't solve the problem. Where were members of the marriage committee? Where were members of the church councils? The purpose of conflict resolution is to restore not condemn. Let's be objective and use God's wisdom in resolving strife in a church setting.

HOW TO HANDLE STRIFE IN MARRIAGE

I have written some points on how to avoid strife generally in Chapter Three. Apart from using the principles listed, there is a need to understand the source of strife in a marriage. Strife can creep into a marriage through many avenues. We need to understand the source of strife and must resolve them quickly. Not all marriages will run smoothly. We each have cultural and varied differences and handle challenges differently.

I will mention four fundamental points that can ruin your marriage and their remedies.

Adultery/Infidelity

If one or both partners are not faithful in marriage, there is bound to be strife in the home. No man or woman wants to share his or her spouse with a third-party. Every man or woman wants marital security and a sense of belonging. Nothing destroys a marriage like infidelity. it is a serious matter before God because you are trading and defiling the temple of God and He promises to destroy such fellows.

1 Corinthians 3:17, *"If any man defiles the temple of God, him shall God destroy; for the temple of God is holy, which temple ye are."*

The fear of God plays a vital role in dispelling the power of infidelity. The fear of the Lord is (and causes you) to depart from evil.

Some preachers claim that a man cheats in his marriage because of a lack of sexual satisfaction from his partner. That is not true. It doesn't matter if a partner is sexually satisfied or not, he or she will still cheat if they don't have the nature of God in them. It is the power of the Holy Spirit and a love for God that makes a man or woman depart from adultery.

Proverbs 16:6, ***"By mercy and truth iniquity is purged: and by the fear of the LORD men depart from evil."***

Besides taking physical measures to avoid temptation, including avoiding careless and close relationships with the opposite sex, both partners should grow in the knowledge of the word of God by continually guarding their hearts. Both must be determined to shun ungodly living and be ready to live for God. By doing that, strife can be resisted when it knocks on the door.

Financial Matters

Money is another cause of constant quarrelling among couples. It is important to discuss financial matters as this will help you both make better decisions in the family.

Though financial sufficiency in a home brings some level of happiness and stability, money, which is a spiritual thing, has the capacity to ruin a home if not handled with care. Every man must be capable of providing for his own household. As the Bible says, a man that cannot provide for his family is worse than an infidel.

Handle money with care, have yearly budgets, and let your wife be involved in financial decision-making. This is because generally women are wiser, futuristic, and better at handling cash than men.

Some men believe that money is for spending. The family as a whole should realize and agree that all money is not for spending. Allow the Holy Spirit teach you to be financially disciplined. You can get my book, YOU TOO CAN BE RICH. It will help you.

Luke 15:14, *"And when he had spent all, there arose a mighty famine in that land; and he began to be in want."*

Proverbs 21:20 (TLB), *"The wise man saves for the future, but the foolish man spends whatever he gets."*

Family Pressure/In-Laws
Let me be honest with you, your in-laws are crucial and an integral part of your home, especially in an African setting, and they must be handled with ultimate care and wisdom. No partner wants his family to be treated shabbily. Both of you have to walk together and strike the balance in your mutual or financial obligations to them.

Let the boundaries you set be applicable to both parties.

Never allow your extended family to be part of the decision-making process in your home. It has never happened in my family and it will never happen. Don't subject yourself to them for settling disputes; rather, channel it to your pastor or a neutral person. Remember, every family wants to protect or take sides with their own.

No single member of our families has ever interfered in our affairs. To the glory of God, in almost twenty-five years of marriage, we only had one dispute that we couldn't resolve amicably within ourselves. We were younger at the time and, by God's grace, the dispute was settled by our pastor.

Infertility/Childlessness

If both partners are not mature spiritually, as the marriage grows without a child, it will bring constant strife and even divorce. Most especially when the extended families are involved. Couples must seek solutions early if there are infertility problems. Apart from solely depending on God for a miracle, it is not a sin to seek for medical help while trusting in God.

The Bible says in the last days, knowledge shall increase, and technology has improved greatly lately to the point where a couple's infertility problems can be solved medically. This should be embraced and used to our own advantage, and believers must not be left behind. There are testimonies of twin births, triplets, quadruplets among unbelievers. How much more you? A child of God? It should double in the camp of believers.

Some couples, especially believers, do not seek medical help on time. In my opinion, I recommend you start medical treatment after twelve calendar months of non-pregnancy, especially if the couple are not staying apart.

After three or four years of marriage without a child, couples should go for adoption to avoid anxiety and worry. This will create family harmony and happiness between the couple. After adoption, let your quest for the miracle child continue. Afterall, all believers are adopted children of God through our Lord Jesus Christ. (Galatians 4:4-7)-

HOW TO MAINTAIN HEALTHY AND HAPPY RELATIONSHIPS

Maintaining healthy relationships either with a spouse, siblings, friends, business partners, or otherwise requires a lot of commitment. Successful and healthy human relationships require effort. Things will not work if you don't play a vital role or work them out; just as the word of God will not work for anyone until they work it out.

Though relationships have their ups and downs, you can do some things to keep them from going under. I am going to give some tips that could help you in a marriage relationship as well.

• **Express Your Love Regularly:** Love is not quiet. Love speaks. Learn to give your spouse praise and compliments whenever he/she is doing well. Women, especially, love to be praised and adored whenever they do well. No woman wants a silent lover, and that includes me. Although my husband is an introvert, a quiet man who hardly talks, while I am an extrovert, I want him to express his love and affection for me on a regular basis.

Express your appreciation and compliment to your partners on the spot whenever they make things happen. Let them have a sense of belonging. God Himself appreciates and is touched by our praises.

• **Respect Your Spouse And His Family:** Let your spouse and his family feel respected. Give honour to them and a helping hand whenever you have the capacity to do so. The way you treat and honour them will be the way they will fight for you whenever you have a problem with your spouse. Respect is reciprocal; it is give-and-take.

Never take each other for granted. Manage your crisis in your bedroom and not with family. Whenever any issue cannot be resolved in your bedroom, refer to church leaders if possible.

• Be Sensitive To Your Spouse's Feelings And Needs: Help your partner with house chores whenever he/she is not too strong enough. Men should learn how to cook for the family once in a while as fun. My husband does that regularly. He studied in Europe and doesn't behave like an African man; whoever gets to the house first takes over the kitchen. He cooks a lot.

• Maintain The Same Bedroom All Through Your Lives: No matter how big your house may be, never have separate rooms from your spouse because love, intimacy, and communication will begin to dwindle. Issues can be resolved quickly when in the same bedroom. Some individuals have separate rooms under the pretext of study or being alone with God. You can have a big family study room. Divorce or separation easily begin when you and your spouse both have separate rooms.

• Go For Regular Vacations Together:
Apart from spending quality time together in the home, relationships can become deeper and sweeter when you make a habit of taking regular vacations either monthly, quarterly, bi-yearly or yearly. It may not necessarily be outside the country. My family does this a lot.

I travel with my husband yearly outside the country while we have a monthly retreat locally. Love is celebrated and our differences deliberated upon and ironed out during this monthly retreat. It can be an avenue to deal with some issues. New ideas can be initiated and it could be a time to plan.

• Be Honest In Your Dealings: Lasting relationships require integrity, sincerity, and fairness in your dealings. Shun infidelity and ungodly dealings. Be open to your spouse concerning any income coming into the family and take decisions together.

• Practice Giving: A life of stinginess is a life of total failure in marriage. Be generous to each other. Relationships are like a plant that needs to be treasured and watered. You do this through giving and care. I do a lot of shopping for my husband, especially when I travel to Europe. Do the same for your spouse.

• **Embrace And Practice The Characteristic of Love:** I refer you back to Chapter Two. Meditate on it.

• **Sex:** Sounds ungodly? Sounds dirty? Don't pretend. Regular sex will lead to more affection in the family and boost your relationship. Sex is good, sex is healthy. It builds a long-term relationship, especially when done in a legal marriage. When you take sex out of marriage, you are planting destruction into your relationship.

Sex is not only for procreation. It is for the betterment of a couple and aids a lasting and long relationship. Never use it as a weapon of retaliation, but use it to resolve issues. Sex makes a partner feel loved, secure, and have a sense of belonging.

• **Praying Together:** Most importantly, set up a family altar to destroy the plans and purposes of the devil over your union. Don't allow him to mess up your relationship. Resist and bind him, asking him to take his dirty hands off your marriage or any other relationship that is precious to you. There are spiritual wickedness in high places whose intention are to control the marital affairs of people. Taking the shield of faith, resist them vehemently.

• **Shun Pride:** Pride is a forerunner of destruction. Nothing destroys a relationship or an individual faster than pride. Never allow ego and pride to keep you from asking for forgiveness when you err. Strife and contention exist easily in the bosom of proud people.

• **Avoid An Individualistic Approach:** Respect God's mathematical approach: one plus one equals one.

• **Effective Communication:** Communication is key in any successful marriage. Keep lines of communication open. It is dangerous when a spouse has to rehearse, treading carefully, before they can communicate to their partner on a particular issue. Couples must develop effective communication in problem-solving.

Don't allow your home to be boring by not communicating with your spouse regularly. Some husbands get offended and irritated when their wives provide useful suggestions on any family matter. You had better listen to your wife!

Women are oracles, futuristic, planners, savers, advisers, full of ideas, and graced with the needed knowledge to move the family forward than men. I am not saying you should one hundred percent agree with women all the time; but, for a successful union, it is advised to constantly communicate your decisions with your spouse.

CHAPTER EIGHT

PRAYERS TO FORGIVE THOSE WHO OFFEND YOU AND CONFESSIONS

I f you have been hurt by somebody or a group of people, you can lay the offense at the feet of Jesus once and for all by praying these prayers. After that make a daily confession (I have included a list below). By doing this, the word of God will be engrafted into your spirit to love again.

David told us to hide the word of the Lord in our hearts so we will not sin against God. The word has the ability to cleanse you of any bitterness and offence that clogs your heart.

John 15:3, *"Now ye are clean through the word which I have spoken unto you."*

In John 17:17, Jesus prayed for the purification of the disciples by the word; *"Sanctify them through thy truth, thy word is truth."*

Keep on confessing until you have the witness in your spirit that you have forgiven the fellow.

PRAYER

Father, in the name of Jesus, I come before you to lay all offenses at your feet in obedience to your word. I refuse to hold anything against anybody.

Since I know that unforgiveness, bitterness, anger, malice, envy, evil speaking against anybody are weights that will slow me down in my Christian race, in accordance with the authority of your word, I lay aside every weight, and the sin that so easily entangles or besets me, and I run with patience the race that is set before me. (Hebrews 12:1)

According to 1 Peter 2:1-2, I equally lay aside all malice, all deceit, hypocrisy, envy, and all evil speaking. As new-born babes, I desire the pure milk of the word, that I may grow thereby.

Today being *(Date* ....*)* at *(Time* ....*)* I am forgiving those who have offended and hurt me badly in any area of my life. *(Write the name(s) of those you want to forgive)*:
1)
2)
3)
4)

Today, I lay all the offenses at the feet of Jesus right now. From the bottom of my heart, I forgive .... *(Mention names again).* I promise not to use the offence against them in Jesus' name.

I lay down my heart before you to be cleansed from resentment and negative feelings toward .... *(Mention names again).*

Your word says, "If I confess my sins, you are faithful and just to forgive and cleanse me from all unrighteousness." (1 John 1:9)

Therefore, I confess my negative reactions and abusive words toward .... *(Mention names again).*

In any area I might have judged him/her/them, I ask You to forgive me. In any area I have kept malice or spoken bad words against .... *(Mention names again),* Father, forgive me. Right now, I receive abundant grace to forgive, to love, and more importantly to bless.

I declare and decree he/she shall be blessed with the blessings of the Lord. Please Lord, have compassion upon them as you have mercy upon me.

I pray you will heal every wound he/she might have inflicted in my life because you promise to restore health unto me and heal my wound. (Jeremiah 30:17)

Father, today I declare and decree that every broken relationship that strife and unforgiveness have destroyed shall be restored in the name of Jesus.

I honour the blood of Jesus by choosing to forgive at this hour; therefore, I walk in the victory and power of forgiveness.

As from today, God's purpose and His standard shall become my desire. I will love what you love and despise what you hate. So help me God.

DAILY CONFESSION TO WALK IN LOVE TOWARDS GOD AND HIS PEOPLE

After laying offenses before God, it is important to know that the devil may still bring offenses to your memory once in a while. You need to resist him vehemently; this is why it is important to keep on declaring the following words to yourself and your destiny. In doing so, you will be able to live the perfect life God desires for you.

CONFESSION

1. I am born of love and I walk in love.

2. The God-kind of love rules my life.

3. I subject my emotions to the word of God.

4. Father, thank you for giving me a new heart and putting a new spirit within me to love You and Your people, you promise to take the heart of stone out of me and give me a heart of flesh. You have put your Spirit within me and caused me to walk in your statutes, and I will keep your judgments and do them. (Ezekiel 36:26-28)

5. God has not given me the spirit of fear, but of power, love, and a sound mind. (2 Timothy 1:7) Therefore, you spirit of fear, I reject you in Jesus' name.

6. I have great peace because I love your law; nothing shall offend me or make me stumble. (Psalm 119:65)

7. I put away all bitterness, wrath, anger, clamor, and evil speaking, with all malice. I am kind to people, tenderhearted, and forgiving even as God forgave me. (Ephesians 4:31)

8. The love of God is shed abroad in my heart by the Holy Spirit that is given unto me. (Romans 5:5)

9. I thank you, Father, because my love abounds

more and more in knowledge and in all judgement. (Philippians 1:9)

10. I am not going to allow myself to be offended at anything anymore. I am not touchy, fretful, or resentful. I take no account of whatever anyone has done to me.

11. I love, I am kind, I do not envy, I do not parade myself, I am not puffed up, I do not behave rudely, I do not seek my own, I am not easily provoked, I think no evil.

12. I do not rejoice in iniquity, but I rejoice in truth. I bear all things, I believe all things, I hope all things, and endure all things. My love never fails. God is love. I am born of God, therefore I am born of love. (2 Corinthians 13:4-8)

13. I thank you, Father, for the peace of God rules in my heart. (Colossians 3:15)

14. I put off and purge myself from anger, wrath, malice, blasphemy, filthy communication out of my mouth. (Colossians 3:8) Therefore, as a new creature and elect of God, holy and beloved, I put on tender mercies, kindness, humility, meekness, long-suffering I bear with others and I forgive them. If anyone has a quarrel against me, even as Christ forgave me, I, ... (*Mention your own name*), forgive them.

15. Above all things, I put on love, which is the bond of perfection. And the peace of God rules my heart, to which also I am called in one body.

Appendix

PRAYER FOR SALVATION

Heavenly Father, I come to you in the name of Jesus. Your word says *"Whoever shall call on the name of the Lord shall be saved."* (Acts 2:21)

Therefore, I confess you as my Lord and personal Saviour. I equally confess you as my Healer and believe in my heart that God raised Him from death. Accept me as your child. From today, I will follow you all the days of my life.

Satan, I renounce you completely to follow Jesus. I am saved, born again, redeemed, and precious in the sight of Jesus.

Amen.

PRAYER FOR THE BAPTISM OF THE HOLY GHOST

Lord Jesus, now that I am born again, I come to receive your gift of the Holy Ghost.

I come boldly, thirsting for the infilling of the Holy Spirit. Your word says I should ask and it shall be given to me. You also said ***"If ye then being evil, know how to give good gift unto your children: how much more shall your Heavenly Father give the Holy Spirit to them that ask him?"*** Luke 11:13

Therefore, I boldly ask you to fill me with your power of the Holy Ghost now. I thank you because I have received it by faith in Jesus' name. Amen.

Begin to thank Him and start speaking out any utterance that God gives you immediately, not your language but that of the Father which the Holy Spirit has given to you. Give those utterances a loud voice and don't allow them to slip away. It may not be fluent in the beginning but it will be perfected sooner or later.

Keep praying in the Spirit on a daily basis and keep studying the word of God to nurture your spirit.

I WANT TO HEAR FROM YOU!

If you are blessed with reading this book, let's hear your praise report. Share your testimony or comments with me through the following mediums:

Email:
funkesagbuwa@yahoo.com;
perfectlove@yahoo.com

Telephone Number:
+234-80331-54148,
+234-70430-05558
(Calls/Texts/WhatsApp)

+1(469) 321-6344
(WhatsApp Calls or
WhatsApp messages only)

You can connect or follow
Pastor Olufunke Simbo Sagbuwa
on social media via the links below to receive
the undiluted word of the finished work of
God and stay updated on activities
related to her NGO
(Turnaround Life Foundation).

Facebook

https://www.facebook.com/funkesagbuwa
https://www.facebook.com/pastorfunkesimbosagbuwa/
https://www.facebook.com/Turnaround-LIFE-
Foundation-112667323425168/

Instagram

@pastorfunkesagbuwa

YouTube

Pastor Funke Simbo Sagbuwa

Twitter

@funkesagbuwa

∿ YOU TOO CAN BE RICH ∿

Many Christians, due to misconceptions, lack a proper understanding of what true riches are really all about - its location, components, uses, and how to access it. They accept whatever level of riches they find themselves on and conclude it must be from God. The result? They end up living below God's ordained standard for their lives simply because they do not or cannot access the dividends of redemption. Hence the purpose of this book.

True riches are for those who have revelation knowledge about them, and this book, **YOU TOO CAN BE RICH**, will open the eyes of your understanding to your inheritance in Christ Jesus, your covenant rights and privileges, which are your kingdom entitlements. You will discover the hidden riches that will change your story and place you among nobles.

The author relates her personal experiences and reveals biblical principles on how to put thieves and robbers that steal your riches to flight and how to find yourself on the Glory Level God has ordained for you.

YOU TOO CAN BE HEALED

Some religious people believe that sickness and disease are natural and a part of life considering we are human beings. With these erroneous beliefs, they therefore accept whatever comes their way. Life is spiritual. God is still healing His people. The Bible says "My people perish for lack of knowledge." Healing is the children's bread and there is a balm in Gilead.

The author, **Olufunke Sagbuwa,** relates her personal encounter with God and how she was miraculously delivered from the spirit of infirmity and death through the help of the Holy Spirit. Topics she covers include

- How to fight a good fight of faith.
- How to overcome the fear of sickness and disease.
- How to reverse curses of sickness and disease.
- How to use the authority of the Word and the name of Jesus to recover what belongs to you.
- The mystery of the Holy Communion and how to take it in your homes.
- Daily healing confession scriptures to stand upon to receive healing.

YOU TOO CAN BE HEALED is a book that will expose you to the reality of your dominion over sickness and disease. Jesus became our substitute on the Cross and He has purchased our healing.